SAM HYMAN

Across the Water, Below the Wind

First edition

This book was professionally typeset on Reedsy.
Find out more at reedsy.com

Contents

Author's Note...

Contained within these pages are a collection of my memories and excerpts from my journals, which have come together, finally, to form my story, with me in it. But not the me now. The 23 year old me: it took a while to write. I thought it would be fun to write it down. It was, it just took longer than I thought. Back then I went on a bit of an adventure (I'm still on it now). I would like to say the usual stuff - that some of the places and names in this adventure have been changed for various reasons.

As for dedications, first and foremost would have to be to the most amazing person in my life, Sabrinah. Also for my three monkeys. You could say that this story is, in part, *how I met your mother*. And to my parents, who, right from the start, never stopped believing in me, the choices I made, and my ability to turn it all into a book.

And thank *you*, for taking the time to read it.

Preface

Salty air. That now familiar smell entered my lungs in the stifling heat, as the crude wooden floorboards creaked and groaned underneath the weight of my feet. Copious amounts of sweat were dripping down my burnt red face and off the end of my nose, made worse by my ridiculous state of overdress. My feet were clenched tight by ill-fitting unpolished worn black leather shoes. (It was my mother who gave me them, since, despite being a supposedly responsible adult, I had no other suitable footwear. She had taken them from my father's wardrobe; I doubt he ever noticed them missing.)

Wrapped around my forehead rested a *segal* – a thick, heavy, colourful woven cloth that sat upon my head like an out-of-place turban. This clashed with a sickly green polyester suit, also ill-fitting, that no one with any sense of fashion would wear anywhere. Least of all here. On top of this, tied across my chest, were two *tinggol* – wide beaded straps - that told stories in the form of beautifully woven images.

I stopped for a moment as I reached halfway across the bridge, now swinging slightly in a welcomed breeze that swept across the estuary before me. My eyes fell upon the mangrove swamps, slowly being overcome by the gently swelling river below, teeming with life and noises that were now a part of my everyday soundtrack. I squinted up at the clear blue sky, in defiance of the intense brightness around me. I smiled. It felt like forces that had been at work since I was a child were now coming together, ringing in my ears and permeating my very soul. I had reached a major point in my life. Right here, right now, I was on the right path, and everything I could see around me was telling me just that.

"You know what?!"

Walking in front, Pawai turned round to look at me. His words broke my reflective state, and I caught him grinning at me, as he always did when he had an idea.

"You are standing here on the bridge that you built only a few months ago," he went on, with that knowing twinkle in his eyes, "and all of the things that have happened to you here must seem strange, you know? You should write a book about this! You have an amazing story to tell!"

He stepped back a few paces, and, holding my camera, he took a photo to capture the moment. Those that were following me across the bridge were caught off-guard, and didn't get time to squeeze in to the picture. I looked at him and grinned back. He was right. Here I was, sweltering in the intense heat, dressed in these strange garments I could barely pronounce, standing across the water, below the wind - and like my *tinggol* that crossed my chest, I had *my* story to tell.

Thanks, Pawai.

Physics & Neville

(Two years earlier)

My beaten up VW Transporter van trundled past the brightly coloured field of corn like a discarded shopping trolley with wobbly wheels. No matter how I willed the damn thing to go faster, the stubborn rattling diesel engine was already working flat out. I was pressing the accelerator so hard I was sure that at any moment my foot would go through the van's rusting underside, and several inches beneath the road surface itself. Nope. No faster. Ah well, Physics is a bummer. My A Level teacher Mr. White never quite inspired me enough. I never saw the point in shining torches through prisms, or stretching springs with weights named after some guy who liked eating apples under a tree.

I decided to study the subject because, well, I wasn't really good at much else. I grew up watching my dad build weird things in his workshop, which had blinking lights, smoldering smells and, when touched, contained enough current to make my hair even more frizzy than it was. But I did learn a thing or two - other than 'don't touch anything with wires' - and started to build things of my own. Normally what follows statements like these, are a list of things which I successfully built. Not much, sadly. But I can offer an amusing anecdote at least. At the impressionable age of 16, one of my first real job interviews was for a post at Hanslope Park with the Foreign & Commonwealth Office. Before finishing my A levels, this would have been a ticket out of school, straight into work. My two older siblings already worked for them, and were having very successful careers there. Naturally that inspired me to do the same.

I sat in the interview room - a cosy office with three elderly gentlemen who all wore heavy tweed suits, themselves sat in an arch around a coffee table in front of me. I was asked all kinds of questions you might expect which were related to the post being advertised. They were particularly interested in my passion for building gadgets made out of my dad's left over circuit components.

"Tell me about one of the gadgets you built," asked one guy, showing genuine interest.

"Well, since I cycle to school most days, I decided to build a theft alarm for my bike. I made it fit into a 35mm film case which could be strapped to the frame of the bike," I declared. "Once I switched it on, it would use a tilt switch to sound the alarm if the bike moved."

"Oh, fantastic! Did it work?"

"Yes, it worked great. Unfortunately my bike got nicked before I was able to fit it."

The office erupted into fits of laughter. I was glad I tried, but that employment pathway was clearly not meant for me. Mine, for now, was to continue with my education.

So I did, and after much sweat generally associated with A levels,

I achieved an embarrassing grade 'N' for physics. I still have no idea what an 'N' means, except that it lies somewhere between an 'E' and *fail*. With my other two more successful A levels in Maths and Art, it was just enough to get me accepted by the University of Bradford, on an Engineering degree. That is what took me up to beautiful Yorkshire, and post degree, fate put me into the aforementioned white van passing the fields of corn near Pontefract.

So, driving as fast as I could get the vehicle to go, with the knowledge that I wouldn't reach my destination – good old John's Organic Farm – any quicker than the speed of light, didn't bother me today. Because something had happened. I was ecstatic. The seed had been planted. It was like I received a wake-up call that my whole being had been waiting for, for years. This was a pivotal moment. The van even acknowledged the moment, and sped up unusually. I overtook a red Ford Escort with glee, thinking my white rust bucket had gained power. It kind of did, since both cars were now going downhill. Physics again. *Gwavity and fwiction*, I heard Mr. White say, complete with spittle.

I approached the sleepy town of Ackworth slightly earlier than usual, ready to fill my van with John's organic vegetables to deliver to the residents of Leeds. Cucumbers and beetroot were the last thing on my mind however. Because that morning, I had had a conversation that got it all started.

It was at Seb and Bro's house, earlier. The door burst open, and in came my estranged looking friend Sebastian, wielding a pristine blue file, which contrasted with his usual scruffy, grubby trousers and slightly ripped lumberjack shirt. The conversation in the kitchen between myself and Seb's younger brother, Bro, came to an abrupt end. We had no choice but to look in Seb's direction.

"Guys! Check this out!" Grinning, he placed his file down on the kitchen side, opened it, and pulled out some sheets of paper, waving them about in the air.

I have in my hand a piece of paper... If Neville Chamberlain was a skinny, milky-white, oil-stained, ginger hippie, then this would have been a classic Kodak moment. My camera would have to wait. I put that thought away and filed it somewhere, eager to concentrate on the moment. Sebastian continued, full of gusto.

"Man, check this out. We have got to apply for this. There's this thing called Raleigh International or something, and they're doing a trip to Malaysia next September – but get this – it's just for young people from Leeds. We only have to raise five hundred quid. It's normally over two grand!"

"Malaysia? Where's that, again?" I found myself asking, being generally clueless about the world and what it had to offer.

"It's all here, dude." He laid out the papers on the sideboard.

So Bro, Seb and I read the information that brought about such enthusiasm. I knew Seb well, and when something inspired him like this, it would usually catch on to me as well. Bro was getting the bug too. That was it. We were applying for this thing. Words and phrases jumped off those pages at me. *Primary rainforest, 33°C, rural communities, jungle trekking, mountain climbing*. Raleigh International, and Seb, had sold the idea to me. I had had no experience of anything like this, but something inside was forcing me to go head first into it and get the ball rolling.

That day at the farm, John the farmer was watching me load his vegetables into my van, laughing. "Eee, Sam! Whats put a spring in your step today, lad?"

"I dunno...I just feel good today, John! Maybe its all these organic vegetables I've been eating!" I knew I was going to Malaysia. I just knew it. Seb, Bro and I all applied, and soon after, we heard by mail that we were invited to an 'assessment weekend', to be held in a forest near Hebden Bridge. The first selection stage had begun!

Porridge & Bile

A sound.

"Urrrrgggghhhh!"

My eyelids were heavy and did not want to open. Not now. Please. They had only been closed for two hours and the sound I had just heard was not what I wanted to hear. The rancid smell of stomach bile mixed with packet noodles added to this unpleasant scenario. Then my worst fears. I felt the warm touch of something wet on my hand, which had somehow found its way out of my pathetic wafer thin sleeping bag. For a moment, the warmth was quite welcoming on this cold February night, but then I came to my senses. I shot out of my sleeping bag, forgot there was a tarp only three feet above me to keep the rain off, slipped and fell right into the lovely vomit puddle that my new team mate Peter had just brought forth into the world.

"Ahh...Sorry, man," Peter groaned shamefully, wiping his mouth on his sleeve. Before I could reply, we heard some shouts in the distance. I recognised them belonging to one of our assessors, urging us to move fast.

"We gotta go, man, come on!" I urged.

I looked around and saw the rest of my team already putting

on their water logged boots. As I joined them in the stress of getting myself ready for fear of failing the assessment if I was last up, I glanced at my watch. 3 AM. The other teams by now were already running round the field like gormless zombies doing star jumps, hops and running on the spot. I had no choice but to join them. Despite all this, I was loving the head-on challenge that Raleigh was putting us through, in a freezing cold forest. I was at this time an absolute exercise health-freak, training in Chinese martial arts most nights. That had definitely changed my outlook on things like this. So, I gleefully jumped and bounced around this field, wiping Peter's bile off my cheeks as I went. Our assessor, a former soldier named Nick, was shouting at us, addressing us by the numbers we had on our bibs.

"Number five, pick it up! Number eight, do you actually *want* to join this expedition?! Come on you sleepy bunch! There's enough time to sleep when you're dead! Keep moving! That's it, number four! This is lovely, you'll thank me later!"

After getting warmed up, Nick told our small group that our breakfast had been 'dropped by helicopter' in the local area. He smiled an unforgiving smile and threw us a map, a torch, and some co-ordinates.

"If you don't find your breakfast, you go hungry. You only have until 6AM, then we are on with the rest of the day."

Food was the last thing on my mind, but I knew I would need that bag of porridge, whether it had landed on a haystack or in a cow pat. A grueling day meant I needed the energy. It was just a role play exercise, but even if there was no helicopter, the rest of it was real enough – if we didn't find our supplies, the day ahead would be much harder.

Luke warm oats mixed with water had never tasted so good. Although I didn't know it, this bland dripping slop that congealed before you could get it to your mouth was to become a regular meal once on the expedition itself. On a *good* day.

I looked around our group as we eagerly wolfed down our food before the sun rose that morning. We were a real mixed bag. There was me, a van driver delivering vegetables to help pay the rent, a paramedic named Jake from Leeds General Infirmary, two students, Julie and Dave from Leeds University, Dev and Ali, a couple of younger kids from Chapeltown fresh out of high school, a couple of other college students whose names I no longer remember, and oh yes, there was Peter, the chunder champion who had just finished his A levels. Nick was watching us from the side, looking at us tucking into this slop, as if it was a top notch meal. He started to tell us that we should hurry.

"If you're in Malaysia, stuck in the jungle, behind schedule, you'll have no time to eat. Get used to dropping your breakfast and grabbing your bags! Don't think I'm making this up, this kind of thing happens a lot."

The rest of the day consisted of bridge building, problem solving and getting cold, wet and hungry. Nick was good at making it real for us, and although our assessment weekend was controlled, safe and tame compared to the real thing, it was a challenge for those not used to it. We all bonded as a team really well – and afterwards Seb and Bro reflected that they had had a similar experience in their teams.

The next few weeks were a waiting game. I willed my application form to the top of the pile, to be chosen to go. I knew the expedition was well over-subscribed, but I had this gut feeling I was going to be on that plane in September the following year.

It wasn't a major surprise when I opened the letter; confirmation that I was accepted on the expedition. That morning, Seb and Bro received the same. We were all off to Malaysia!

The weeks and months leading up to September consisted of a mad rush to get all the necessary equipment we thought we would need. Raleigh Head Office kept recommending to buy loads of stuff from various camping shops. So, those with money bought all the expensive equipment and those of us who were stubborn, skint or both got our gear from the local army surplus shops.

Although the majority of the expedition was funded thanks to a great Raleigh team of staff, headed up by Isabelle who later received an MBE for her work, each participant still had a target fund to raise themselves. We did this as individuals and groups, and I loved every minute of it. My fund raising consisted of washing cars in the freezing cold car park of the NHS offices in town, with fellow venturer Marc. Our hands turned blue at the end, but we did a good job shining all those cars. Ironically many years later Marc became somewhat of an NHS hero, leading the corridors of his department at Leeds General Infirmary during the pandemic of 2020.

Next came pulling a vintage bus through town, whilst running around amongst the bemused public, shaking buckets of money at them. It was an odd gimmick, and I don't know who came up with the idea, but it beat sitting in a bath of porridge or beans. Abseiling forwards and backwards off a bridge somewhere south of Sheffield, and doing a 30 mile hike across the Brecon Beacons in Wales were other activities which raised money through sponsorship of friends and family. The Beacons walk was particularly tough, but a fantastic experience. Our group got lost for a while, though we found the intended trail again. I did the whole trail in my Doctor Martens boots, which was a big mistake. Those things are not designed for long walks. It was a lesson to learn, and a reminder to buy some decent hiking shoes.

Goodbye & Hello

On the day of the departure, I sat in my room in Harehills, fundraising complete and all equipment bought. It was now time to pack all my stuff into my backpack. I had everything laid out on the floor. How the *hell* was I to put all this in my bag?

2 canoe bags

Full set of clothes x 3, suitable for hot weather

Evening set of clothes - long trousers and long sleeved shirt, to avoid mosquito bites

1 bandana

3 essential oil bottles

1 notebook

1 mess tin

1 bottle of herbal insect repellent

1 mosquito net

Toiletries – razor, toothbrush

1 sleeping bag

1 sleeping bag liner

1 pair of sandals

1 pair of hiking shoes

1 head torch

1 camera
4 bungee cords
1 huge army poncho, which could double up as a tarp
Zinc tablets
Sun cream
6 months supply of Malaria tablets
1 bottle of homeopathic tablets, to combat the effects of Malaria tablets
Sunglasses
Extra t-shirts, underwear

After pushing it all in, sitting on it, bouncing on it and pulling tight all straps, I was ready to put the damn thing on my back. There was supposed to be a 20K limit on luggage. All I can say was that it was a good thing no-one checked.

My next challenge was to get to Seb's house to meet Seb and Bro, before going to a sending off party held at the Leeds Civic Hall courtesy of the Mayor. My trusty van was left at John's farm - a dirty big white diesel van left on the road always attracts unwanted attention - so the idea was to get the bus. The problem was, if there was a bus to Seb's house from mine I didn't know about it. I looked at my watch. I was late. There was nothing for it but to start on a long walk/jog up Harehills lane. The rush of the whole expedition finally starting was setting in, and I feared my friends would leave for the Civic Hall without me. Once I arrived, I saw to my dismay that the brothers grim hadn't even packed. There they were sitting down watching TV. Being organised wasn't their strong point. After stressing, shouting, and several expletives, we were finally all ready to go. We all stepped out of the house, buzzing with excitement.

Once Seb locked the door, I decided to take a photo. *The boys, ready to go.* Seb's bald head reflecting in the sun (he shaved it all off to raise money), and Bro sweating in an oversized jumper. That photo, captured the feeling we all had – a great sense of adventure, mixed with "we can't wait to get out of here". The timing for all three of us couldn't have been better.

The sending off party at Leeds Civic Hall seemed to go on for hours. It was a laugh though. A fellow venturer named Jane brought in her own samba band, causing mad echoes around the huge function room that had been prepared for us. After a long session of dancing the night away, and a sending off speech from the City Mayor, it was time to go. Coming out of the building at that time, the city steps were covered in flowers left there in tribute to Lady Diana, who had tragically died only three days earlier. That had a huge impact on the collective emotion of the UK public, but one we were to miss completely – even Elton John's accompanying hit *Candle in the Wind* had finally blown out by the time some of us returned to British shores.

It was dark outside, but fairly mild considering it was early September. The coach soon arrived, and it was time to load up and find a seat. Lots of people had come to this departure point. I felt detached and indifferent – nearly everyone had their girlfriends, boyfriends, siblings, mums, or dads. You name it, they were all there hugging and full of emotion. I'd never been into that goodbye stuff. The expedition was only for three months. What was the fuss about?! Not that any of my family could have seen me off anyway - they all lived miles away in the south.

I glanced at my watch. 1030PM. It was an overnight coach trip straight to Heathrow. I decided to set it eight hours ahead to Malaysian time. That way I'd be more prepared. It was 630 AM in Malaysia right now, so I thought I'd stay awake for the whole bus journey, adjust to the new time zone.

I fell asleep before we passed Sheffield. What a lame ass.

* * *

I looked down the aisle. It seemed as though we took over the entire plane. A sea of turquoise 'Just for Leeds' Raleigh T-shirts (travel shirts we had to wear), generally being obnoxious, rowdy, and for some, air sick. I walked down to the end of the plane to stretch my legs. Poor Malaysia – look what's coming your way! Walking over to a window at the back, I gazed down at the world below. We were passing the Alps. For me at that time, it was quite a spectacle to be seeing those mountains without actually venturing into them. I had only ever been on a plane once before, when I was sixteen. At home I would always stare at atlases for ages, picturing myself going through different countries. Looking at the real atlas, I saw that it's landscape was both bizarre and beautiful, especially looking down on it from high up, on a clear day such as this was.

We stopped off at Dubai, a reasonable halfway point. It was night time when we arrived, but we were hit by the temperature as we stepped off the plane. The searing night time heat was a teaser for what was to come. After another eight hour flight and dipping in and out of some very welcome sleep aided by a blindfold, we arrived in Malaysia at last, early morning.

Eager to press on, I was first out of the airport after collecting my luggage. I walked out of the airport terminals in Subang Airport, Kuala Lumpur and felt the heat wave again, albeit a different time of day. It didn't bother me so much this time. I walked straight towards a waiting crowd of nineteen Malaysian venturers, identifiable by their *Raleigh International Malaysia* black t-shirts, who were to be our companions for the next ten weeks. I shook hands with all of them, and was greeted with smiles, hello's and *welcome to Malaysia*! I was struck by how amazingly friendly and smiley these people were, especially this early in the morning!

After a very brief but welcome breakfast of baked beans and egg in a youth hostel nearby, we headed for Kuantan – home of the Raleigh Expedition HQ – on the opposite side of the peninsular. This was going to be a long bus journey.

Once on the bus, I sat next to Saini, one of the Malaysian venturers. After finding out that we would be working the same project together, we struck up an instant friendship. I wanted to find out more about this country and its people, and Saini was just the guy – it was like sitting next to a tour guide as we passed through the very hazy city of Kuala Lumpur. He was good at it, and he had the experience – Saini's day job was cabin crew for Malaysian Airlines.

"The smog is terrible isn't it? It's from the fires in Indonesia. They burn the forest, smoke comes up here."

I looked out of the bus window and saw a busy city teaming with life, smudged out almost by this thick dirty haze. I later learned that the air pollution index at this point was so bad, that there was a rumour that the local authorities stopped publishing the figures for fear of putting off tourists. We were on the outskirts of the city centre. I could see these huge skyscrapers that dwarfed everything else. Long spikes appeared *above* the clouds themselves – my eyes followed a faint line downwards, revealing that they were attached to two towers coming up from the middle of this mad city centre. I pondered this unusual structure that looked as if it were about to collapse, causing more dust and smog.

"The Petronas Towers!" Saini correctly guessed my thoughts. "This is our icon. They are the tallest building in the world," he said proudly.

As I looked at it, it certainly seemed fit for an icon. The Malaysian President Dr. Mathadir wanted to build something famous for Malaysia and get it more recognition. To an extent, it worked – he had got two architects from the US to work on a tower each, to work competitively to reach the top, thus be the first to break the world record for the tallest building in the world. The building process broke other records also, due to the many problems the workers encountered, which included pouring thousands of tonnes of cement to make better the bad condition of the ground. *Lumpur* in 'Kuala Lumpur' means *mud.*

"But what about that building over there – it looks taller!" I pointed at an oddly shaped tower nearby that looked like a giant javelin, with a slowly revolving disc at the top end.

"The Menaros Tower! It's not taller; it's just on a hill. If you measure the tower from its base, it's shorter than the twin towers." Saini changed the topic of conversation to the expedition, and our first project we were to embark on. We were off to Sabah, Borneo. This was another two and a half hour journey plane across the South China Sea. Saini informed me that Sabah was a very different place to Peninsular Malaysia. Before that though, we had a few days of jungle induction ahead on the peninsula, and this would begin after an uncomfortable few hours bus ride away.

Lost in my thoughts, I found solace in gazing out of the bus window, grateful for its ability to open. My eyes widened with amazement as a mesmerizing spectacle unfolded before me—an endless procession of motorbikes, outnumbering the cars by far. Each rider had a flimsy plastic helmet with no strap, and a jacket worn back to front. The zips were flapping wildly behind their backs as they weaved in and out of the traffic.

Further on, as the smog and the haze fell behind us, the more rural side of Malaysia presented itself. Majestic palm trees and dense jungle emerged, painting a lush panorama. Fleeting glimpses of the occasional villages went past my window, run-down shacks or wooden huts perched precariously on stilts. A few open air restaurants & cafes – which sometimes seemed to outnumber the houses – and some small stalls dotted the roadside here and there.

Having absorbed a wealth of information from Saini's guidance and my own keen observations, exhaustion finally caught up with me. Despite the bus's cranky disposition and the unevenness of the road, I finally surrendered to slumber.

And so, I experienced my first dream in the heart of Malaysia—a dream that would set the stage for the extraordinary journey awaiting me.

Spiders & Spirits

Rudely awoken by the juddering brakes, I opened my eyes to find that the bus had pulled over by a large white house with large areas of well-kept grass, which was then surrounded by masses of jungle. This was field base for Raleigh International, the place where operations ran to manage all the projects we were to embark on across Malaysia. Some of the Senior Team stayed here. One of them, Mr Tang, was in charge of the accounting for each project (and the holder of everyone's money). He later earned the title *Lord of the Ringgits*. As well as collect our pocket money in-between projects, it was also the place to pick up our supplies before each project was to begin.

There were a huge amount of supplies for our first projects. Although I was grateful for the little sleep I did get, I was not looking forward to loading our buses with three weeks worth of rations and cooking equipment, radios, tools and medical kit. I think we were all on auto pilot, but eventually we managed the arduous job of squeezing everything on board. The aisle right through the bus quickly became full of boxes and barrels. Health and Safety had slightly different boundaries here. We promptly left, and began the long trip to jungle camp, not far from Kauntan itself. We knew that this would be the time for our 'training'.

As I wearily stepped off the bus for a second time, the sun was still burning down on me, though I didn't know how many hours had passed. I was completely dazed and felt like someone had drugged me and put me on a strange bus full of odd people. And I *chose* to do this?! Pondering this, I stood in the lay-by, next to the edge of thick jungle, I watched the side panels of the bus being inched open by the driver, revealing our supplies and belongings. I donned my backpack and, like everybody else, took what I could and then marched my first few steps into the dense jungle, as directed by voices of the expedition staff.

I felt a certain tension from Saini as we passed into the darkness of the jungle, and did not really know why – after all, he was a Malaysian and should be used to this. He began looking around nervously, unsure of his footing. As we carefully progressed through this mad place, I looked around and couldn't believe my eyes and ears. Strange insect choruses echoed from everywhere, enveloping us in a cacophony of sound. A mass of wild green was all around, there was no semblance of order. The wilderness reigned supreme, save for the narrow trail we cautiously followed. Sweat was pouring off me even more as we made our way through. Eventually, we reached a clearing, where the trees gave way to a cluster of large purpose built log cabins perched high above the ground, on stilts. In the middle of this beautiful natural environment, we found our way to a scout camp, big enough to house over 100 people that made up the expedition.

"I guess this is home for the next three days!" Saini concluded, with that sense of nervousness still present in his voice.

The next couple of days consisted of our jungle training – anything from extra first aid, building a radio antennae and using the radio, making a *basher* to sleep in (basically a rectangular hammock design, complete with mosquito nets and tarp covering), digging in temporary toilet holes and all the associated sanitation guidelines, and filtering water for drinking (far from the toilet areas!). By far the most enjoyable bit of the training was the river crossing exercise. These rivers were very deep, with a flow that looked calm, but were misleading at best. In these situations, we had to take off our packs and tie them all together to make a 'raft' of 4 bags. The purpose of which was to immerse ourselves into the river, whilst holding on to the raft as if it were driftwood. It was times like these I was grateful for the canoe bags inside, keeping all my belongs dry. Surprisingly, it worked.

As we got to the other side of the river, we were told that during the jungle trekking phase, such crossings would be common place, and unexpected. What could be a trickling stream one day could be a raging torrent the next: such was the nature of this part of the world. The rainfall effected everything.

All of these exercises were a great chance to get to know everyone in our first project group. There was a bit of relaxing at the end of each training day, and holding of talks and presentations about getting acquainted with local customs. Naturally, some of the Malaysian venturers I had met at the airport were leading these talks, including Saini.

There were many do's and don'ts in this culture. *Apa kahbar* was the main greeting (and the first Malay words I could speak), and only use your right hand to shake (gently) with. Do not shake a female's hand, unless she offers it first, which is unusual in Malay culture. Do not express anger in public or cause anyone to lose face. Always take off your shoes before entering a house. Treat food respectfully – don't leave a tin of beans on the floor, or step over it, even if the tin is unopened. There were many more points made, and at the time, it was hard to take it all in. Here started a real learning experience of other people and cultures, something which has always fascinated me. I decided to get closer to these local Malaysian venturers, to learn more. I was intrigued.

The next night, we had trekked further into the jungle, leaving the scout camp far away, to experience setting up our bashers and sleeping rough – to prepare for the bare basics once the projects started. No scout hut this time.

And so it was that I found myself sat with the Malaysians in my first project group – Azira, Saini, and Minnie. Our bashers all set up, it was time to chill. We talked long after everyone had retired to their bashers, sitting around a small fire, lit for the light it gave and the smoke it gave off. Smoke would keep many, but not all, of the insects away.

I sensed the nervousness of my three new colleagues, as well as feeling it myself. The jungle we were in was a scary place, especially in the night time. My imagination constantly played tricks on me. Snakes, spiders, tigers, elephants...they seemed everywhere in my mind, dancing in the shadows caused by the flickering of the fire. I questioned this anxiety I sensed in the others too.

"This place is not meant for people. We shouldn't really be here," explained Saini, "We have to be very careful and respect the surroundings, the jungle...it's not our place. It's not our home. We are guests."

"Many people here believe that the jungle is occupied by spirits, not just animals," Minnie went on, describing a fundamental belief across South East Asia. "This place has never been occupied by human beings, and there is much we don't understand about what goes on here."

Great, I thought, *something else to be afraid of.*

"I'm not sleeping here tonight! I won't sleep!" Saini declared, "I'll wait for a couple of days until I'm too tired to be scared!" His deep nervous laugh echoed round the trees surrounding our camp fire. I realised we were all up, awake, talking to each other just to keep our eyes open. Who would be the first to sleep? I couldn't understand how easy it seemed for the others in our group to fall asleep so fast (I later found out that due to the same fear, hardly anyone else actually slept!).

Soon after, our small die-hard group finally made the move to the bashers. I climbed in, and slipped uncomfortably into my sleeping bag liner, on the green canvas suspended between two trees. It seemed strong enough. I tested it earlier. It lay underneath a blue tarp which I had tied above in a v-shape, forming a roof. I had smeared vasoline around the tied bands secured to the trees, as this was supposedly meant to stop the hoards of ants from invading you in your sleep. As for spiders, snakes, leeches and scorpions etc., I just had to hope.

That night, I heard a couple of thuds as some bashers collapsed to the ground bringing their occupants with them. No one helped. We were all too scared. These were the bashers that we were to build and sleep in throughout most of the expedition. If they collapsed whilst we were in them, it was a learning experience. Get up, rebuild and retie. These things were essentially *home*...for the next ten weeks. As I lay there my overactive mind raced on. What the hell am I doing here?!! I tried to forget thinking about furry eight legged creepy things, or slimy forked-tongues licking my face. Let alone the angry spirits of the jungle! If I was going to be bitten, stabbed, scratched or possessed to *death* then I had to be prepared. Somehow.

I turned on my side, uncomfortable now, and desperately still, not daring to twitch any of my incredibly tense muscles. *If I move, something will happen. I'll disturb the wild life. I'll anger the spirits and they'll get inside my head and really mess me up. My basher will collapse and I'll land on the jungle floor, having to ward off leeches and scorpions.* It wasn't getting any better.

Time dragged on slowly. But then it got far worse. My heart actually stopped. *What the hell was that?!* I felt something *move* against the side of my body. Something between my ribs and the green canvas. I jerked and rotated rapidly in the narrow hammock like a fish flapping on the deck of a boat. *My hand! My hand!* I was lying on my hand, it was my own fingers twitching against my side. *I was scared of my own hand!* I nearly fell out of my own basher! This was my first proper night in the jungle. How the hell was I going to survive ten weeks of this? I tried to let it all go, close my eyes and somehow get some sleep.

But no, the night was not over yet.

My heart stopped for the second time that night. This time, it was no limb of mine - it was a scream. Not an ordinary scream you might hear, but a very real, very intense and desperate *call for help* type of scream. The terrifying scream of none other than Ralph Johnson, two bashers across from me.

"AAAARRRGH! SOMEBODY HELP ME!!! THERE'S SOMEONE HERE! SOMETHING'S JUST WALKED UNDER MY BASHER, I SWEAR TO GOD!!! SOMEBODY HELP!! JESUS, THERE'S SOMETHING HERE FOR CHRIST SAKE!! HELP!! "

Ralph was in my group. I didn't know him so well yet, but he was friendly, very talkative, and very skinny, with a crop of blond hair on his head. Before joining the expedition, he was living in and out of homeless shelters in Leeds. He was always honest and genuine, and on the spectrum. He later became known by the locals as 'Matata Vogok', a term used by an indigenous tribe in Borneo, once they met him and drank rice wine with him. Basically, it was an affectionate term which means *crazy pig*.

As his screams echoed across the entire National Park of Malaysia, I was certain that there wasn't a monkey, elephant, scorpion, orang-utan or human being within a 50km radius that *didn't* hear him. And I was next to him. In his group. His *friend.* The reason that I did not move a single muscle (and instead tensed all of them up even more), was probably the same reason that all of the other *brave* and *adventurous* members of the expedition didn't either. The entire situation was terrifying beyond belief. However, our distinct lack of assistance to a friend in need did not fairly reflect how much we all liked the guy, or how well we worked as a team. Enough said, I think.

Destination Sabah

Jungle Camp consisted of a few days, and had finished with a quick visit to Kuantan's Sports Complex, where we were to prove to our expedition leaders that we could swim 250 meters for health and safety reasons. Given the kind of stuff we had been through, I couldn't help but notice the irony in any of this. Unfortunately in my case, before joining the expedition, I had very little ability to do anything in water but drown. I was one of the crap kids at school that was always given a float or arm bands. However, in the weeks leading up to the expedition, I had a friend, Craig, who was an expert swimmer. He trained me up in Beeston Leisure centre to do breast stroke for a few lengths. The fact that I no longer sank, swallowing half the pool with me, had been a massive improvement. Craig earned a few beers with that one.

The problem was, now we were being asked to do this in an outdoor pool in the blazing sun at high noon, temperatures soaring. Exposing my bright white body to the aforementioned weather conditions, I quickly got in the pool. The sun was the most intense it had ever been, reflecting off the water too. My eyes narrowed to slits in order to see. There was nothing I could do except go for it. Thinking my position on the expedition was in jeopardy, I stretched out and kicked off. It felt like it took forever, and as each minute went by I changed from white to pink to red. I remember getting to the other side a few times, but didn't keep count of my lengths. I'm sure I died in that pool, but somehow 250 meters later a new burnt version of me climbed out, with the coach, Nick, watching, ticking his clipboard.

"Well done number five!" he grinned, remembering my bib number I wore back at the initial assessment trials.

Once the swimming trials were over, we gathered into our groups for our first briefing for Phase One, given by Lorraine, our first project manager. Kampong Longan Besar, Sabah, was our destination. It was a remote village community (*kampong* meaning 'village') in the Kudat district in the north part of Sabah. It was also home to the Rungus people, an indigenous group of people in Borneo, whose main source of income was subsistence farming and fishing. Here we were to repair an existing 150ft suspension bridge and 350ft attached walkway, which extended over an estuary and mangrove swamps. The existing bridge, we were told, was on the verge of collapse and provided the only means by which the village children could walk to school, or anyone really, just to get into the nearest town. It was the life line of the village - crossing over the water in hollowed-out canoe style boats wasn't as practical for them. The project aims were to survey the damage, rebuild the bridge and its foundations, whilst interacting and learning from the village community. Basically, to live among the locals and experience a whole new way of living. In three weeks.

"And," continued Lorraine with a huge smile, "the village is next to the beach! The most amazing beach you have ever seen... and it's deserted! No one on it, save a few of the village children.

This really is an amazing place: I've been lucky enough to see it all already for a risk assessment before you lot got here."

She was grinning wildly. She definitely believed that this was the best project on the whole expedition. And who were we to believe any different?

* * *

Every rose has its thorn of course, and this meant getting up at a ridiculous hour to catch a plane from Kuantan to KL, and from KL to Kota Kinabalu (or KK as it was known) in Sabah. And so our small team of fifteen expedition members left the rest of the Raleigh gang behind in Kuantan to start the journey. Minnie, Azira and Saini made the Malaysian contingent, with the rest of us from Leeds. I felt good about the group, and had struck up a good relationship with Bella, Ant and Lucy. Bella was very bubbly, had a mass of curly hair much like myself, and was one of the easiest people to get along with. Ant worked as a joiner back in Leeds (very useful as we were building a bridge) and loved to sing Michael Jackson songs very badly. Lucy always had an infectious grin on her face and could cheer you up at a moment's notice. Our group also consisted of a few others, including the presence of the aforementioned Ralph, who was proving to be quite a character, and a very tall chap named Karl, who would constantly quote Star Wars films and pretend he was a Jedi. He got on well with Nigel, a lad who had just finished high school. This was our group. *Group One.* It was a great group, and in the years that followed, many of us have still kept in touch. We got on the plane and headed for Sabah for the first ever time, and slept soundly for that three hour flight.

On arrival, I was feeling exhausted like the rest of the group. We clambered down the stairs from the plane, and walked across the tarmac, our first steps in Sabah. It was early morning, the sun was beginning its climb, shining its beautiful rays in a lovely clear sky. As I walked across the tarmac, my feet started tingling, I could feel a connection with the ground beneath me.

Finally. You are here.

A sense of peculiarity washed over me, leaving me bewildered. Why had that thought just entered my mind? The feeling lingered as I boarded the airport bus. It felt like I had arrived at a place of profound significance. Not the home I knew back in the UK, but here, in Sabah, a place on the other side of the world I had never heard of, let alone been to before. Yet, an uncanny familiarity tugged at me. Blurred recollections, fragments of distant memories, began to resurface—a mix of childhood daydreams, perhaps, spent gazing at the clouds in the playground. Something was connecting with me. I was being rewired. And in the midst of it all, everything just seemed... right.

Seated on the bus, I eagerly poured out my thoughts into the pages of my journal. Scribbling away, I sought to capture the essence of these seemingly irrational thoughts, in an attempt to unravel what was going on.

The bus journey from Kota Kinabalu to the Kampong was one of many mad journeys to come. Once again, I found myself aboard a relic from the past, a bus at least half a century old, devoid of any semblance of suspension or comfort. And yet again it was a journey that took hours. Saini sat at the front of the bus, talking to Avoi, our hired driver. Avoi was a diminutive local man, donning a cap reminiscent of a bygone communist era, who possessed an uncanny affinity for voicing complaints about virtually anything. He was ranting on loudly about something to Saini, and though I couldn't decipher a single word, I gathered that he was fervently protesting about something. We had been driving for what seemed like hours, and he wouldn't stop. Eventually, Saini turned around, with a look of exasperation etched upon his face.

"The driver says he doesn't want to drive all the way to the village!" he explained. Lorraine's facial expression changed immediately.

"What do you mean? This is where we are supposed to go! We're supposed to get there today, we have a schedule to follow!" she protested. Saini shifted uneasily.

"Avoi here says it will be too dark by the time we get there, and we cannot arrive after dark." Apparently it was taboo for any guests to arrive at such a late hour. Daylight was the time for such arrivals – especially a bus load of strangers.

"Also, there is no electricity or any lights, and he will not know where to go! He suggests going to Kudat, and then to the village the next morning," Saini continued. This seemed to make sense to Lorraine.

"Right. OK. Kudat it is then," she gave in, "we'll find a hotel somewhere and go from there." Of course, this meant paying the bus driver more for his time. Avoi was happier once we agreed.

Much of the rest of the journey was in darkness anyway, with windy bumpy roads, and again many large animals wandering across the roads, which delayed us even more.

When we arrived in the town of Kudat, it was quite late. Lorraine, resourceful as ever, secured our accommodation at Hotel Kinabalu—a modest establishment tucked away up a stairwell nestled between two unassuming restaurants. With check-in formalities swiftly taken care of, we wasted no more time, and immediately went back downstairs to take part in a new found hobby in Malaysia: eating Malaysian food in a Malaysian restaurant.

The Bridge

I woke up raring to go, despite yet again having little sleep. After a brief breakfast in the same restaurant as the night before, we boarded the bus once more. It was then that I learned Avoi had slept in the bus through the night, to keep an eye on his vehicle and our cargo for the project. Being so tired, it was easy to forget important things such as keeping your entire luggage and all the project equipment safe.

Our bus continued down an unusually smooth road out of Kudat for some time. The roadside quickly became jungle, palm trees, and the odd small building or house.

At long last, Avoi steered the bus to a halt beside a humble shop nestled along the roadside. It looked very run down, and there were very few other buildings or dwellings around. Upon entering, I could see that it was packed from floor to ceiling with boxes and boxes of household goods. Anything from chocolate bars to soap. Although this shop appeared to be far from anywhere, this I guess was the Sabah version of a regular corner shop. Lorraine obviously knew where we were.

"OK guys, this is your last stop before we enter the village, so if you want any personal supplies, now is your chance!"

The entire group got out and exchanged what little Malaysian dollars we had for 'Cloud Nine' chocolate bars and tins of Milo. The very small but happy owner of the store just kept smiling as his sales figures for the month just trebled, on account for our bus load of foreigners.

As we returned to the bus I noticed a small dirt track that headed off the main Kudat road we had come along, which ran into a mass of palm trees and jungle on the right side of the road.

"About 30 minutes on that road and we're there," Lorraine explained, pointing in the direction of the track.

The bus moved very slowly to avoid the holes and rocks, not really suitable for a vehicle with already balding tyres such as ours. The road was no longer a road, by anyone's standard. Though I could not understand his rantings, I could tell Avoi was not happy about taking his bus down this track. With calculated precision, he skillfully rocked the bus, navigating massive bumps and dips, wheels spinning in the mud occasionally.

The view became more interesting now. Trees as far as the eye could see, over a beautiful hilly landscape, with paddy fields dotted here and there. Now and again there would be the odd solitary house on stilts, looking like all it needed was a nudge to bring it crashing down. Half an hour later, a breathtaking moment unveiled itself before us. The track veered sharply to the right, and as if revealing a precious secret, the most awe-inspiring sight materialized on our left—a vast expanse of the bluest sea, lapping onto what seemed like a deserted untouched beach. Every head on the bus turned in unison, faces grinning as wide as the open sea itself. Ant was the first to comment on this amazing sight.

"This village had better be close – I've got a lot of sunbathing to do!"

I noticed on the other side of the track we were driving on, there were a few of these raised up houses, just perched on the edge of the jungle, forming a line between that and the beach on the opposite side. I caught sight of one or two children running about around the houses, excited with the sight of our bus trundling past. Chickens were waddling around here and there, pecking at the ground.

For a few minutes more, the bus followed the narrowing track, and headed right again, where the path abruptly ended. We disembarked, eager to look at our surroundings, but also just to get off the bus and stretch. There was a small wooden shelter with a bench by the side of the road. It was like a sort of bus stop. Behind the makeshift bus stop was a huge estuary, which then opened out onto the sea which we saw just moments ago. Looking to my right, on the other side of the shelter, I saw the beginnings of wooden walkway, which started as a ramp at ground level, and rose up to about 6 feet off the ground. Staying at this height, it led off into the distance through mangrove swamps either side.

"Whoa...this is the bridge we're supposed to rebuild?! I didn't think it would be this big!" Saini exclaimed.

"No, that's only part of it – there's more, but you'll find that out in a minute!" Lorraine replied.

Just then a figure appeared at the far end of the bridge, walking slowly towards us. As the figure came closer I could see that it was a thin elderly lady, draped entirely in a weathered, patterned cloth, once colourful but now bleached and faded by the sun. Her face seemed very much the same; skin that had seen endless sunny days. As she came nearer she smiled and began muttering something to Minnie, who was squinting as if finding it difficult to understand what was being said. By this time I only knew about 5 words in Malay, and I didn't hear any of these.

When the lady had finished talking, she turned back around, ambling off into the direction she came from. Minnie, understanding the significance of the encounter, took it upon herself to relay the unfolding situation.

"Well, I'll tell you what I *think* she said! This woman speaks Malay with a strange accent, and I didn't get half the words. She is the Chief's wife and has gone to inform him of our arrival. She says the bridge isn't safe to carry things on, and that we should bring our equipment and bags in by boat, so she will summon some of the villagers to come and help."

"Great – that'll make things a lot easier", started Ant, "everyone just chill out until help arrives!"

Chilling out in the intense heat was difficult. I decided to venture under the bridge to find some shade. It was here that I realised just how noisy the surrounding swamp land was. It was teeming with life – buzzy insects, beeping, clicking and croaking everywhere.

"This place is *awesome*!" exclaimed Karl, who followed me for the sensible shade. "And we're gonna spend three weeks here? – sounds good to me!"

"YOW!" I cried out suddenly. I felt a sharp pain coming from my left foot.

"Woah! What happened dude – a bite already?" Karl asked.

"I think I've trodden on something," I answered. Sure enough, I lifted my foot up and saw a sharp old nail protruding out of an old piece of wood – part of the bridge that had since come loose, probably. This nail decided to go straight for my big toe. I *knew* I should have kept my boots on – sandals are all very well in this weather but they expose your feet to things like this. No tetanus shots here, I thought.

By this time, there was some commotion by the side of the bus stop. I could see that two boats had arrived, behind the shelter. People were already loading some bags into them. This would take time – the boats were just hollowed out tree trunks in the shape of canoes, albeit quite large ones. Another wider boat came by, that had the look of a typical row boat you get in parks back home. Lorraine instructed some of us to go on ahead into the village by carefully negotiating the bridge, whilst the rest of us remained by the bus shelter, to go in by canoe with the equipment.

As my turn came, an empty canoe drifted in once more, steered by one of the villagers – a young lad wearing sunglasses and a big smile. He immediately began to load some bags into the boat. As I stumbled in myself, my new village friend started to row, and continued his massive smile.

"Hi! My name is Anjas. Tony Anjas! Welcome to my village!"

"Hi, I'm Sam. This is an amazing place!" I replied, looking around at the most spectacular view.

We were where the river widened and opened out into the sea – on one side, towering hills cloaked in untamed jungle, that stretched out to the edge of the water, forming one side of the bay. On the other side of our river was nothing but more swamps and jungle. Anjas, steered us away from the beckoning allure of the sea, leading us deeper into the labyrinth of mangroves. Here, the river narrowed as it meandered around a bend, revealing two distinct paths. One was a narrower lane, veering off into a thicket of dense mangroves, while the other widened into a grand expanse, an open waterway that extended into the distance, stretching as far as my eyes could see. It was just like I imagined the Amazon river to be.

Spanning across this wider expanse of the river, like a delicate thread connecting two worlds, stood the bridge that had brought us to this village. *Us? Rebuild that? You must be joking*! I thought. I could see some of my team members carefully crossing the bridge – wobbling and swaying in the breeze. It reminded me of that Indiana Jones movie with the scene of the rope bridge that Harrison cut in the middle to escape. Thankfully, this one not spanning a huge chasm of certain death.

Anjas steered our boat into the smaller lane, and the bridge soon disappeared out of sight. The mangroves came tight around us.

"Sam!" said Anjas, his grin still present, "My English not very good – but you teach!"

"Yeh, no problem!" I smiled back at him, certain that I would find time to teach my new friend. Part of the project was to socialise and work with the villagers themselves, so I looked forward to this part.

"Ha Ha! *Aso Masalah*! No Problem. *Aso Masalah*!" he replied, as he sped up his rowing.

The boat went round another corner revealing the first sign of a settlement of people. A wooden shack stood precariously on the edge of the bank, patched up with biscuit tins and sheets. It looked like a shed made out of a patch work quilt. The river narrowed again and revealed the edge of the village. I could not believe my eyes. My heart was pounding, and a funny feeling came over me. I felt like I'd been here before. That same feeling I got at KK airport.

Anjas brought us to the muddy bank in between two huts. I

was in absolute awe of my new surroundings. I got out of the boat and walked up from the bank. The houses were dotted around in small clusters here and there, all raised off the ground on stilts. Many had rusted corrugated tin rooves, some had thatched grass of some kind. It was a sudden hive of activity, like I have never seen. A few young kids were running about, playing, some hiding in the shadows of their houses. Adults too, swinging in hammocks underneath the houses, or sitting in groups murmuring and chatting away. Some women were sat around weaving baskets or making fishing nets. In the distance I could hear someone going about their work – an axe, chopping away at some wood, banging of a hammer onto metal. Underlying all that was the constant chattering coming from the mangrove swamps at the edge of the village, from which we had just come. As I looked around I could see that this village was surrounded by hills on each side, covered in nothing but lush jungle, like it was some sort of secret paradise. Where on Earth was I? No roads, no cars, no signs of anything that I could say was normal. It was as if I had stumbled upon a realm far from the familiar constraints of the world I once knew.

"Come, Sam" prompted Anjas, snapping me out of my gawping. He led me past a few dwellings to where the rest of my team were now gathering – by a long hut, covered in peeling blue paint, fading in the sun, next to one of the houses ahead. In front of the hut, was a wide open field about the size of half a football field. This field was the central point of the village; on the other side of the field were more clusters of houses, about a dozen or so. As I looked closer, I noticed that the field was in fact a football field. It had two bamboo goal posts at either end! I put my bags down with the rest of the equipment already there, and caught up with the rest of my group standing around the entrance of this long hut.

"Right, then!" said Lorraine, "This is it, guys. This is where we'll be staying for three weeks. It's beautiful, isn't it?!"

I could see that everyone else was just gawping like me, taking it all in. What a bizarre place we found ourselves. You couldn't get more of a culture shock than this. Some children were gathering around our group. We were certainly a spectacle.

"They've even got a football field!" cried Nigel, one of our group, who just noticed the bamboo posts. I could see that he would be well settled here, then.

Ant instructed that we should place all the equipment inside the hut, out of the way. This was done albeit lethargically; the past few days were taking their toll on the group now. Azira explained that the blue hut was some sort of community hall, used by the villagers for meetings and guests. This was where we were staying, so we each found some floor space inside to sleep for later. It was just one big room surrounded by a wire net for windows. It was also very hot inside, so once we placed our things, we quickly went outside again, finally able to relax.

I could see some villagers staring at us from a distance, chatting away timidly, and giggling. Occasionally some of the braver children would run up to us and say something that only our fellow Malaysian venturers would understand.

"They're laughing at you hair and your skin!" explained Azira, laughing, "They think its really unusual, because they haven't seen this before."

One of the children started saying something else. By this time some of the other villagers began crowding around us, and the outside of the blue hut became what felt like the focus for the entire village.

"This child wants to know what these are!" laughed Minnie,

pointing to my arm.

"Freckles," I replied, smiling at the young girl, who came closer and suddenly reached out to squeeze my arm. She was fascinated by my skin, seeing it change colour as she applied pressure like I was some kind of life size toy doll. She found this hilarious and did it again. Karl, Ralph and Ant were also getting similar attention being mobbed by groups of kids that couldn't have been older than four or five years old. It was fascinating, but weird, to be such a spectacle.

Minnie then became engaged in a conversation with a couple of adults who approached. One of them was a short plump old man wearing a brightly coloured cloth wrapped round his head like some kind of crown. He was dressed in a pale blue collared shirt, with smart slacks in a slightly different shade of blue. As he stood there talking to Minnie, I realised something protruding from the corner of his mouth. It looked like a rolled stub of tobacco. Next to him was a taller gentleman with a very serious but friendly face. Much thinner than the first, but also dressed relatively smartly. I noticed he was wearing a pair of black shoes, that despite being scuffed and wrinkled, still gave him an air of importance somehow. In contrast, the plump guy stood barefoot, his weathered feet splayed across the grass as if wearing anything on his feet was a ridiculous idea.

Minnie turned to our group and introduced them to us. The man with the head cloth was Mr. Apaun, the village Chief. The coloured cloth around his head indicated his position, and was something he wore at all times. The taller man was Mosuta, the district officer of the village. Chief Apaun and Mosuta smiled to us all and said something none of us understood. We took it as a 'welcome' and thanked them both. Both sides were laughing at the fact that language would be a huge challenge for us all, even for our Malaysian team mates. We would be liaising with Mosuta throughout our bridge-building time here. The Chief would take on the responsibility that we were looked after properly. After shaking hands, we spent the rest of the day chilling out, ready for the next day...our first day of work!

Surun & Milo

None of us had slept well on our first night in the village. It was too much at once to build bashers for all of us, let alone work out a good location for them. The village was in a jungle clearing sure enough, but it wouldn't have been right to wander off and find a place between trees, out of the village. Since we were guests, we had to work with and follow the cultural norms and expectations of our hosts. This meant that last night's sleep was spent in the community hut. It was a large empty room, and like every other dwelling here it was raised up on stilts. The floor was wooden slats, the walls pretty much the same except for a wire grill at head height, which acted as a window all the way round. Even though we were in a building, it was airy, and so we all needed to hang up our mosquito nets above our roll mats. Once we were in and settled with our spot, it took on the look of a rushed emergency shelter for refugees.

Our first full day consisted of sorting out camp duties, getting a roster going for who prepares breakfast and dinner, and establishing with the village Chief and Mosuta where would be a suitable place to set up our bashers. They both pointed to the field. It was to be around the edge of one side of the football field. Mosuta and other villagers got to work straight away, heading off into the jungle and coming back with thick wooden branches. They made a tip on one end so they could be thrusted into the ground as posts. There were four posts to each basher, so we could tie the bed part between them, suspended at hip height above the ground, and secure the tarp above it for the roof. In between that we would hang our mosquito nets. For extra cover, we arranged to put them all in rows, so the feet of one would be at the head of another. The roof tarps would overlap each other as one 'terrace'. Thus our bashers became our home. That tiny stretcher sized area was the only personal space we had away from everyone else, even though we were all squashed together in one line.

Despite our efforts, setting these up required constant readjustment once the rains came. Any drips that formed would have the habit of leaking through somehow. Eventually we got it right, and those beds became very comfortable. On occasion, the rains were so heavy and sudden that we had no choice but to make a run for the community hut just to stay dry. Downpours like I have never seen, meant those bashers didn't have a hope. Remarkably, by the next morning, everything was dry as a bone, as if nothing had happened.

We also had to establish a system for using a toilet behind the community hut. This consisted of a reasonably well kept portaloo which the village had maintained for any official guests, usually council officials from the local town. It was a squat toilet, which was fine, except being in that small portaloo container during the heat of the day was unbearable. Everyday norms didn't exist out here, as we soon learned, and every type of comfort we were all familiar with was a far off distant dream.

Susan, our team nurse, had rigged up an anti bacterial soap dispenser which ruined the skin on your hands, but we couldn't take the chance of spreading germs and getting ill out here.

During the early stages setting up of camp, Ant and a few others went to survey the bridge and the walkway. For the first part of the project, we needed to assess the damage, what the repairs would be, and how to get it on done within the nine weeks that we had. Our group would start the first three weeks, the remaining six weeks would be the job of the next two groups to come after us. Hence, as Ant informed us later that day in our community hut meeting, our main job was to refit the foundations for the other groups to build on. Literally. We had to get it right; the other two groups wouldn't be able to do anything useful otherwise. It wasn't a case of repairing the existing bridge – that was shot. Besides, due to increased tide levels, the water would rise much higher than usual. This meant the new bridge had to be suspended much higher. On top of that, the raised walkway leading to the bridge itself on both sides all had to be re-built. This was a lot of work. Lorraine suggested that in our three weeks, we should only have Sundays off to chill out. A day's work would consist of rising with the sun (sleeping in was impossible due to the heat anyway, once the sun began its climb), and finishing up close before sunset. It was going to be all hands on deck.

With all things set up and ready for a full day's work tomorrow, we all agreed to get some down time at the beach – after all, we had seen it from the bus and couldn't wait to get in the sea. We set out carefully across the broken bridge towards the beach, as eager as kids on Christmas day, to get to that sea. By now many of the villagers had joined us out of fascination, and seemed keen to get to know us, less shy than when we first arrived. We eagerly strolled past the shack used as a bus stop, and headed along a dirt track with a couple houses along the side.

"Oh my word!" I heard Karl call out in front of me, as we walked through a gap in the trees, the ground becoming sandy. The view suddenly opened up to a pristine beach with the sea gently lapping it. The sun, positioned slightly above the horizon, promised an amazing sunset to come. As soon as we walked on to the warm sand away from the trees which separated the dirt track from the beach, the villagers went wild and ran to the sea. This, I soon realised, was their playground. They had this every day of their lives. It didn't take more than two seconds for us to do the same – go wild – and run into the sea as fast as we could. Traditionally for me, stepping into the sea for the first time always came accompanied with a shock. UK waters are always ice cold, even in the summer. The shock this time was different – the sea was luke warm, as if someone just ran a bath. Once further in, I lay back and floated, looking up at the sky. Perfection, I thought. It doesn't get better than this. The sky, formerly bright blue, became hues of orange and pink. The sun was on its way down, and this paradise was the perfect place to see it set on the ocean horizon. It was an utterly beautiful moment for us all.

The next day we set to work on the first part of the walkway section which led from the bus shack area, to the beginning of the bridge itself, further down through the mangroves round the corner. It was a long walkway in a complex environment. Supplies had been pre-ordered from the local town, and we were able to get things underway under the guidance of our carpenter

Ant. Where the foundations were still solid, we were hammering in new slats one by one. Experienced with hammer and nails, Ant was able to bang them in at lightning speed. The rest of us were snail pace by comparison, but it was all good teamwork. Others were working on a separate section, installing newer foundation posts, driving them vertically into the ground. All the while we were sweating away in the intense sun, the noise from the mangroves around us never relented. Strange insects would come and fly close by for a brief inspection. Some more alarming than others, though we were oblivious as to which ones could potentially cause us harm.

On one occasion, a low pitched buzz came close to my ear. I turned to see what it was. Perched on one of the vertical wooden posts was the weirdest looking creature I'd seen yet. The size of a large beetle, standing upright with a strange round body that looked like it was wearing a huge backpack with wings behind it. And it was looking at me. I couldn't see any eyes, but I could feel it looking at me. It jumped off the post and took to the air, seemingly defying natural law, and gracefully floated around. The most worrisome thing was that it moved with a kind of intelligence and purpose. It was curious, and carefully kept its distance, flying about and then stopping mid-air, as if making some kind of surveillance report.

"Holy shit! That's something straight out of a Star Wars film!" Karl had clocked it too, and on this occasion I fully supported his analogy.

"It's OK – just don't bother it too much!" Minnie seemed to dismiss it calmly. "I've heard about these things. One of the villagers told me – they pack a nasty sting, and will only attack if threatened. They call it a *Surun.*"

"Can you tell it we mean no harm?!" I suggested.

To our relief, the Surun turned its back on us, and decided to fly away. Later that day though, I was alarmed to see that a couple of children had caught one, and tied a piece of kite string around its leg. They periodically released it to fly two or three metres in front of them, until the string went taut. In fits and giggles, the kids would then run around the field with their new toy.

Each morning, we were woken up by two members of the team whose job it was to make breakfast for everyone else. One morning was like no other. Ralph decided the best way to bring the rest of his team into the day was to bang a cooking pot as loud and as fast as he could with a wooden spoon. The variety of language that came out from everyone's basher at 630am was as colourful as the sun rise that day. Nigel, whose basher was at the foot of mine, screamed and cursed every which way he could, and made a pact with God that he would murder Ralph in cold blood. Thankfully, Ralph's breakfast that he made for everyone seemed to placate even Nigel into forgiveness. It felt like a hearty meal to set us up for the day.

After cleaning up the camp, we all got ready to work on the bridge for another day. For me, the morning was a lovely part of the day in any part of the world, but here it was really something special. There was something about that freshness in the morning that was so nice, knowing that in an hour or so the temperature and humidity would rise to levels that made even breathing difficult for some. I made my way with Karl and Nigel out of the village, and climbed the walkway to the main part of the bridge spanning the estuary. I could see a couple of people on the opposite side of the bridge, heading towards us. Treading carefully as we always did (some of the boards were badly weathered or rotten), we started crossing the bridge to get to the walkway on the other side, where we needed to work. The two villagers from the other side came closer and into focus, as we were halfway across the bridge, swinging above the water.

It was then that I stopped in my tracks. The most beautiful girl I had ever seen was approaching me, bag slung over shoulder, carefully walking across the broken slats of the bridge. She had long jet black hair, and stunning dark eyes that looked straight at me. She slowed down and smiled at me. I fell to pieces. Her smile broke me, I was helpless. I wasn't sure if my mouth was open or closed, but it was certainly of no use – I was unable to utter anything. She didn't speak either. For that moment, I felt that I was looking at a face that I have known all my life. I had no idea who she was or where she came from, and yet there was some kind of connection, familiarity, that I had never experienced before. She held my gaze for a while, and then shyly looked away.

"Hey, Sam!" Karl's voice pierced through the moment, and startled me. I heard a chuckling coming from Nigel.

"Mate....are you gonna let this lady pass?"

The reality of the situation kicked in. This absolutely stunning lady in front of me was politely waiting for me to step to one side and allow her and her friend to pass. And I was just blocking her way, acting like an idiot. I moved across to another plank to give way. She remained silent, looked at me again, and then stepped past as she was urged forward by her friend standing behind her. I was trying not to be rude, but I couldn't take my eyes off her, until she turned away and continued crossing the bridge towards the village. My body suddenly lunged clumsily to the edge of the bridge, as I felt a sharp punch to my upper arm. Luckily I grabbed the side rail of the bridge and maintained my balance. Nigel was laughing out loud now, and punched me a second time in the arm.

"What the hell happened to you?! Dream boy! You're out with the fairies!"

I didn't have an answer.

"I've got to agree with Nigel on this one," Karl stood there, hands on hips, shaking his head. "You were completely bowled over by that lass. You looked totally under her spell!"

All I could manage was to shrug my shoulders, puff my cheeks, and breath out. The three of us continued across the bridge to start our work for the day. I tried to keep focused, but at the same time tried to process what had happened. Who was she? Most likely someone who lived in the village. I hoped to see her again. I really hoped I would.

The day seemed to take ages to pass, but eventually it did. We trudged back, drenched in sweat from the heat of the day, eager to change and finally chill with the rest of the team. As we reached the edge of the mangroves, they opened up to the now familiar scene of the village, as usual bustling with activity. Hammocks creaking and swinging under all the dwellings, hands and arms dangling from them. It seemed to me that the underneath of each house was used to hang out and chat – sometimes all day – as the children would run about and play games. My eyes searched around for the girl I had seen earlier. No. Not anywhere that I could see.

"Come on, Romeo, lets get changed and get the volleyball on!" Karl knew what I was doing. "Maybe she will be on the field in the village team."

We had played volleyball with the villagers a couple of times already, it was a great way to break the ice with the villagers and get some down time after working out on the bridge. The village team grew each time, as more villagers were keen to take part. Clearly, they were far more athletic and agile than we were.

The game this evening ensued as it usually did, no one keeping score, but just having loads of fun. Despite being exhausted from the day, it was so nice to feel the temperature drop as the sun lowered in the sky. After half an hour, another group joined on the opposite site of the net. And it was then that I saw the girl from the bridge earlier. I wasn't sure what to do – I certainly couldn't say anything, and assumed she couldn't speak English. The idea was to play it cool, focus on the game, and hope that somehow I could get closer to get her attention. However, this was a plan that failed miserably as far as staying focused on the game went. I found myself looking at her most of the time, and not the ball. I definitely became the most useless team member for my side. But it was worth it, I caught her eye a few times, and she stared back with a look that I cannot put into words. There had to be a way to speak to her, but how? I only knew some basic phrases. Asking her *what's the time?*, or, *can I have an iced milo please?* wasn't really the kind of lines that were going to get me anywhere. Clearly, I had to speed up my Malay learning, and it had to be fast. I was only here for three weeks.

Every day in this village seemed to last forever, but in a good way. Our group was gelling really well, and we had a good routine going. When we stopped at the hottest part of the day, we would all congregate in the main community hut. Sometimes we would play team bonding games initiated by Lorraine or Susan, other times we would just enjoy the time to collapse and sleep. On one day, it was Karl's birthday. Unknown to him, Lorraine organised someone to head out of the village into town, to stock up on supplies. At the same time she requested as many different Milo products as possible for him. We had learned early on that this chocolate brand of sweets and drinks that was everywhere in Malaysia, was a much loved product for our Jedi loving friend. To see Karl's face when we revealed a mini-Milo hamper in that hut, was another amazing memory to keep.

The Chief's House

A week or so into the project, we all felt pretty much established and had routines. In the evenings, Ralph used to slip away elsewhere into the village while the rest of us chilled out in the community hut after the days' work. He would come back late, and get promptly back into his basher. I asked him about it one day, intrigued as to what he was doing each night.

"Ah! You've noticed!" he said with a huge wide eyed grin. "I've been hanging out with two villagers called Mainah and Will, in the Chief's house. It's really cool, they are very happy to have me there." I nodded, which he took as a cue to continue. "It's why we're here, isn't it? To get to know the people we are staying with. I don't see much of that happening, so I'm just doing it. I don't understand much of what's going on, what with the language and everything, but it's a laugh. You should join me tonight!"

I did. And I quickly realised that Ralph had done something none of us could so far. He connected with some of the villagers in a way we hadn't done yet. Despite the fact that we were building a bridge here in the village, it was Ralph that built the bridge of friendship to the villagers themselves. He had taken himself night after night to the villagers' doorsteps– and they welcomed him. He consequently became something of a star among them. That first night, as he eagerly led me in the dark to the other side of the village towards the Chief's house, I understood just what a feat this was. There was a delicate balance of knowing what the right thing to do was in a place like this, it was easy to get things wrong and end up in an embarrassing or uncomfortable situation. Ralph had just ambled through all of that, and connected with everyone he met, through his antics of acting like a court jester.

There were hazards we had to be careful of whilst negotiating through the dark in this place. Water buffaloes would be standing around in random places, and avoiding them might mean falling into the bathing holes dug into the ground full of muddy water. Walking close to any dwelling set off the dogs that belonged to it – waving a torch at these animals didn't really have much effect. Ralph had already learned the Rungus word that was the English equivalent of 'shoo' for dogs - *sino!* - and would yell it as we walked in between two larger houses. I could hear muffled giggles as we went by. Clearly some of the villagers were finding it amusing that Ralph was starting to use Rungus words.

As we continued walking through the dark, I could see the area opened up a little. At one edge, I saw the river which ran down the side of the village from the estuary. At the other side of the clearing was a larger house on stilts. I could hear the strumming of a badly tuned guitar, coming from the steps that led up to the house. Ralph led the way, and confidently strode towards the base of the stairs. He rested an arm on the side rail, and nodded towards the figure sat half way up the stairs, with a guitar across his lap. I could see behind him were sat two others. It was dark, but from their outline they had long hair, resting their elbows on their knees and seemed to be listening to the lad with the guitar. He stopped playing.

"Hey Ralph...*salamat datang*. How are you?" He spoke with a soft voice, and laughed when he finished speaking, perhaps, I thought, because he used English.

"Hey Will! I'm good. Very good. Nice to see you again! I've brought my friend, Sam." I smiled up at him. He looked at me and smiled back.

"Well...kom, Sam...*salamat datang*! My name is Will." I replied back with my *salamat datang*, which always put a smile on the people here. They seemed to love it when foreigners tried to learn their language. Will beckoned Ralph and I to go inside, and we all walked up the stairs to the veranda outside the entrance of the house, about 8 feet high, which over looked the rest of the village. I could see several other houses from here, some completely dark – I guessed the occupants were sleeping – and some had the flickering glow of a candle coming from inside.

We took off our sandals and added them to the small collection of flip flops along the side. We knew by now that to wear anything on your feet as you enter a dwelling would be very insulting, and make the hosts feel very uncomfortable.

Will and the two others led us inside the house. Unlike other places we had passed, the room was lit by a fluorescent strip light tacked to a plywood ceiling, which allowed me to see the rest of the place and our hosts. Will was accompanied by two girls, one of whom had very similar features to him, so I assumed she was his sister. The other had a more round face, but with the same striking features that made these Rungus people so different to everyone else. He beckoned us to sit down on the bamboo seats which lined the perimeter of what seemed to be a living room. There was no sign of the Chief or his wife. I assumed they would be asleep. One of the girls quickly laid out big square padded cushions across all the seats. As we sat down rather awkwardly, the girl I assumed to be Will's sister walked to the end of the room and down a step which opened out to a larger, darker room lit by a candle on a table. Will just kept smiling and started playing guitar. To my surprise, I recognised the song by the first chord. Thus began one of those moments when you realise that no matter how far away you travel from everything that you know, globalisation is truly a powerful thing. *Unchained Melody* by the Righteous Brothers was the last song I expected to hear in this situation, but there it was, being played right in front of me. Will had sang the lyrics spot on, word for word, with a very tuneful delicate voice. I hated the song. But here, sat on this bamboo seat in a village in the jungle, the song was a delight. It's funny how perspective changes when you are far away from your own country or culture. When something pops out unexpectedly like that, there is some kind of recognition. And in this case, the fact that someone went to the trouble of learning the whole thing, you kind of had to like it.

The girl from the darker room returned with a tray of glasses, each filled with what looked like a brown chocolatey drink which I assumed was Milo.

"For you...*minum*!" the girl said as she passed the glasses to Ralph and I.

"This is Mainah, my sister," Will explained, confirming my suspicions.

"*Nunu habal*!" she declared.

"*Nunu habal* means *apa khabar*. How are you? Our Rungus language," Will said as he stopped playing his song. "Because we are Rungus, not Malay people." Ralph and I nodded, eager to learn more from our new friends.

"Can you play a Rungus song?" I asked him, interested to know what it would sound like. He understood, and started playing some chords. His playing was like any other ballad song, but as he sang the real difference showed itself. I had gotten used to hearing Malay now, and recognised some of the characteristics involved. What Will was now singing was entirely different. I had heard Rungus before, being in the village for a few days now, but hadn't really focused on it until now. I made a mental note to record this song later, using the small dictaphones each group on the expedition had, for recording audio diaries.

As Will was half way through his song, I heard a few more people coming up the stairs. As I looked up, I saw the girl from the bridge earlier. She came in with four others. They spoke softly with Mainah, laughed, and sat down on the floor also listening to the song. One of the other boys that had just come in sat next to Will, and rested his arm on one of Will's shoulders as he continued singing. These people had much more physical contact than I was used to, especially for male to male, or female to female. This was in contrast to the lack of public display of affection between a male and female.

Will finished his song, Ralph and I clapped. He put his guitar to one side and started chatting to all the others that had come in. I was happy to just sit and listen, whilst trying not to look like an idiot in front of this girl from the bridge that I so desperately wanted to talk to. At this stage there were no introductions, just the occasional glances and smiles. Everyone else seemed far more relaxed than Ralph or myself. Will moved himself from the sofa to join the others on the floor. It seemed they were more comfortable there, so we joined in. Now all of us sat on the floor, despite the more comfy furniture on offer, it was then that we broke the ice and tried to introduce ourselves. Will seemed the only one able to speak a little English. He introduced the people around us. The girl with the round face was Jukina, her friend, Mina. Another boy, named Yokiun, and finally, the girl from the bridge. *Sabrinah.*

I woke with a smile on my face that morning. The sunlight tried its best to break through the blue plastic tarp above my head. It was still cool, but the heat would soon build, and no matter how tired you were from the days work, lying down in these bashers for long was not an option, unless you wanted to know what it was like to die in an oven. But for now, it was ok as I lay there thinking. I knew her name. I finally had some kind of contact with her. We hadn't talked the night before, what could I say? I got the impression she knew no English, and I didn't know what to say in Malay or Rungus. But somehow it didn't matter. I was absolutely mesmerized by the experience, and could think of nothing else. I knew nothing about her, she was a complete mystery to me. It was an intense collection of thoughts as I lay there readying myself to get up and sort out breakfast for the group. I made an attempt to switch it all off. I stood up and stretched towards the sky. Stop this nonsense, I thought, I am 23, what am I thinking? None of this kind of thing is for me, especially someone I don't know, let alone can't speak to. My resistance wouldn't last long though.

Ralph and I returned to Chief Apaun's house each night. It was an excellent way to get to know some of the villagers this way, and we both learned a lot of the culture and language. More importantly for me, I got to know Sabrinah more, and we would often sit together on that floor in the Chief's house, and make attempts at conversation, finding out about each other along the way. This first phase of building the bridge now became something completely different for me. I had to a job to do of course, and got stuck in like all my team members. But my mind was no longer on the bridge. It was occupied with this girl that I hardly knew. Regardless, I continued to work along the length of the walkway over the next few days, sawing lengths of wood and banging nail after nail. Thankfully there was enough going on during this phase one to keep me going. There was never a dull moment.

A Fly In The Eye, & Goodbye

Later one evening, we gathered in the community hut as usual to discuss how far we had got, and what was still needed to be done. It was important that we stuck to our intended time frame so that the other two groups who would come after us could continue the work, and get the whole project completed in nine weeks. As it happened, we were on target, a lot of the walkway from the bus stop shack to the edge of the estuary had been built. The heavy H frames to hold the walkway above the mangrove swamp had taken longer than expected; we had to work for longer hours and have less time off, so it wasn't without the stress of deadlines.

Sat around the perimeter of the hut, we had become a tight nit group. We had done all manner of team bonding exercises that Lorraine had dished up. Some of it had been quite fun. Playing blindfold twister, we had suddenly become kids again. It was a nice escape from the work we had been doing.

Just then our play was interrupted by a shriek. Susan, our team nurse, came running in from outside, covering her eye with her hand. As a couple of us stood up to see what was wrong, she managed to get out the words that she had been stung near the eye. On removing her hand, it looked like she had done a few rounds in the ring. It was already puffed up and red. It was quite distressing to see our own nurse panicking and in a lot of pain. Lorraine attended to it quickly and calmed her down.

Anything could happen here, and we were far from any medical help other than what Susan herself could give. Today was a reminder of where we were, and how easy we could get into trouble. Thankfully though, Susan rested up and her swollen face reduced after she self-administered some anti-histamine. Considering all the things that could have gone wrong during our time here, I think we were quite lucky.

The rest of our time during phase one remained intense, however, in every conceivable way. We worked hard to reach our target, ready for the next group 'Phase Two' to continue what we had started. Ralph's continual antics made him infamous, and although receiving a few stern warnings from Lorraine, he managed to pass out several times from drinking too much rice wine. Memorable evenings of seeing him ride a water buffalo, and even fall into a bathing hole for the aforementioned beast have stuck with us all. He truly earned his title as *Matata Vogok.*

My encounters with Sabrinah were always the highlight of my day, no matter how brief they may be. She would write down words for me to learn. Other times she taught me some local games that were often played by some of the younger children, usually involving sticks or stones. There was definitely some kind of bond forming, and inevitably this got noticed. Random times during the day one or two little kids would come looking for me at the bridge site, and hand me a scrunched up bundle of small flowers.

"This from Sabrinah!" they would declare, to the laughs and whistles of my nearby Raleigh team mates. They may or may not have come from her, but this would continue each day, as an ongoing tease.

As we reached our third week, we were all thinking about how it would feel to leave this amazing place. Many of us in the team had become so emotionally attached, not just to the project and what we were doing, but to the people we had come to know. But it was also a time for celebration. As we got on with finishing the walkway section, and hit the last nail through, we all decided to celebrate by walking along the main section of the bridge, and jump into the river below. However, it was only upon reaching the riverbank on one side, still dripping with excitement, that we were met with the bemused expressions of a couple of observant villagers. Through fits of laughter, they casually informed us that, on occasion, these waters were known to host the presence of crocodiles. In typical Rungus style, they were laughing so much about what they saw, despite the potential danger!

On the penultimate day, the leader of the village, Chief Apaun, came to our group during one of our meeting times at the community hut. He had a pained look on his face, and started talking to us all, even though only Minne, Saini and Azira could understand. He announced that everyone in the village had become sad. Sad in the knowledge that our group had become like family, but were leaving the next day. As Azira translated we all nodded in agreement. We really felt like we had all been taken in as a family, from the minute we arrived. Chief Apaun continued, and we all listened to Azira as she translated into English again.

"Since this is our last night together, you must allow us to give you a sending off party in Rungus tradition. It is very important to us to be able to do this for you. You are all very important to us. You are family. Please come to my house this evening, we will have food for you, as well as *mongigol* and *sumundai*!"

As Azira got to the last sentence, she also looked confused, and turned to Chief Apaun, I assumed to ask him for clarification. He laughed and gave a reply.

"Don't ask me what that those last two things are!" Azira said, "He just told me to wait and see. I guess we are all in for a treat!"

"What do you think it is? Eating peyote?!" Nigel's joke going over the head of most of the group, but got a giggle out of a few of us. Whatever it was, we all looked forward to it.

We busied ourselves gathering our belongings, leaving out what we needed for one more sleep. The bus was to collect us in the morning, so we had to be ready. The rest of that afternoon was time to chill, go on a last wander around the village, or like some, catch up on some siesta time. For me, sleep was the last thing on my mind. I wanted to savor every minute I had left here. I had to find a way to say what I wanted to say to Sabrinah too. My language skills were not yet good enough, so it was at this time that I turned to my closest Malaysian friend, Saini. He was brilliant, and seemed to understand me very well. I wrote a letter of what I wanted to say to Sabrinah, and he translated it to a Malay version, word for word. This process also really gave me a deeper knowledge of Malay too. He, like the other Malaysian venturers, was impressed with the speed at which I acquired the language. I surprised myself, having been utterly useless at French and German in school.

I went out, and found Sabrinah with a few others hanging out as usual under a house, some sitting and swinging on the hammocks.

"Oh, Sam!" Will called to me, in the usual Rungus way, with an *Oh* before the name. "We are all so sad today, you know?"

"Yes, us too, Will!"

"Why you going tomorrow? You should stay."

"We have other work to do. In other villages. But don't worry, I will come back when I finish!" I replied.

"Ah yes! You must come back, ah? Somebody waiting for you!" he laughed, nodding in Sabrinah's direction.

I sat to talk to Sabrinah. Kids were running about under the house, coming up and squeezing my arm again, or asking me to count to ten in Rungus. Never a dull moment here, but never a chance to be alone.

"You come back?" Sabrinah asked, switching to simple Malay for me. I told her I would. That I had to. That our time was too short, and I wanted to get to know her more. I gave her my translated letter. She took it sheepishly, and put it away to read for later.

The conversation changed to what would happen this evening, at the event Chief Apuan spoke of. They all seemed very excited about it.

"It's very good," Will explained, "because we don't often get to have the *mongigol*. Only for special times. But tonight is even more special, because we can show it to foreigners."

I was intrigued even more. They all returned to their own houses soon after, as they had to get prepared for the evening. Not least, to make sure all the food was cooked for everyone. It sounded like it was going to be quite a feast.

As the sun went down one more time for us in this glorious village, we had all got ready and worked up an appetite. Anjas came down with Mainah, to escort us all to the Chief's house.

I wondered how we would all fit in, given the size of our team. We all climbed the stairs of this now familiar house, took our shoes off at the veranda and walked in. The Chief's family had really done some work. All the chairs before had gone, and right through the centre of the room and beyond into the next, was a long table with plastic chairs running along each side. The table was covered in a long table cloth, and had all manner of plates of food all the way along the middle. It looked like a proper viking feast! We were all asked to sit -surprisingly enough seats for all of us, whilst various members of the Chief's family and other villagers stood around or sat in other parts of the room.

"Wow!" Lorraine sat there staring at all the dishes. Big plates of seafood that I hadn't seen before, huge fish delicately laid out on platters, all manner of vegetable dishes. And of course jugs of water, and milo for those with a sweet tooth. It was most humbling that these villagers went to all this trouble for us. It bothered me that they put so much food on for us, clearly these were not people who had a lot of money. And why weren't the villagers sat with us to eat? Will soon explained to me. They had eaten earlier, and besides, this was their thank you to us. It meant so much to them to see us eat well, regardless of the fact that some of us felt uncomfortable eating in front of them. It was certainly a banquet we wouldn't forget.

But there was more to come. As we finished up, we could hear loud gongs banging outside. The Chief's family beckoned us all to step back outside. Once we climbed back down the stairs, we could see where the noise was coming from. In a clearing, they had three heavy looking gongs hanging from a wooden frame by rope. Three elderly villagers were sat on chairs next to each gong, striking the gongs in a rhythmic fashion holding a wooden beater with rubber wrapped around the end. The musician in me soon realised they were playing an odd-time signature, with one of them playing a different overlapping rhythm.

The commotion had drawn a multitude of villagers, now scattered about on plastic chairs, while small fires flickered nearby, their smoke dutifully warding off the persistent mosquitoes. As we settled into our seats, a figure emerged from the crowd and positioned himself near the gongs. It was none other than Anjas, his head adorned with a vibrant cloth, complemented by beaded straps crossing his chest. Wrapped around his waist was a long intricately patterned orange sarong. It was quite something to see. Behind him, were several girls all dressed in traditional Rungus garments - mostly black in colour, with bright threaded patterns. Beads and jewelry were everywhere to be seen. Around their wrists and ankles were big heavy looking brass coils. The gongs got louder, and Anjas spread out his arms wide and high, and started dancing and hopping about. The ladies stood in a line behind him, turning on the spot in a very delicate way, with their hands out stretched and moving up and down. They made a line, like a sinuous snake, gracefully following his lead, their arms undulating in synchronized patterns. It was a mesmerizing display, as the dancers weaved in and out, creating a captivating spectacle of movement. Anjas cried out, "Hooo!" and then hopped and shuffled around. The line of ladies followed him wherever he went, maintaining a snake-like line. This would go on for a while, until Anjas stopped and gave the head cloth to someone else, along with the sarong he was wearing. The ladies all changed places and took turns also. So this was the *mongigol* and *sumundai*. The former, being the name for the male part of the dance, the latter for the female dance. No peyote, then!

"Your turn next!" Anjas laughed as he came by. He wasn't joking either. That night we all got to have a turn, much to the amusement of our hosts. The dancing went on for sometime, and was a great event to finish our time together.

The next morning was not easy. Our breakfast was a more quiet and somber affair, knowing it was not only our last in the village, but our last together as a group. We tidied up the camp, left the essentials for the next Phase Two group, and collected our backpacks to head out across the bridge one last time. As we walked through the village to get to where the walkway and bridge began, we could already see some very tearful faces. Some of the children came running up to us, crying, pulling at our hands. It was a moment for many of the team to try hard to choke back the tears ourselves.

Some of our equipment was taken across to the bus shelter by boat, the way they came in, whilst the rest of us walked across the bridge with our heavy packs behind us. At the other end of the bridge, began the walkway that we, Phase One, had built. Suddenly feeling more solid beneath our feet, this new structure over 6 foot high proudly supported our last walk through the rest of the mangrove swamp, all the way to the bus stop. Many of the villagers were already there, some had walked with us across the bridge for a final farewell. Lots of photos were taken, one in particular was of the whole group sat on the walkway ramp at the end, with Mosuta and the Chief at either side. We also went under the first part of the raised platform - where I had trod on a nail on the first day - and each in turn signed or carved our name in the first strut.

The bus arrived, and did its u-turn to point in the right direction, away from the village. We loaded our bags into the side section. I went over to Sabrinah, who was also visibly very upset. She didn't look out of place - everyone was the same. Ralph was inconsolable. It had hit him really hard, especially not having a family back home. He was really loved here. I couldn't hug Sabrinah, even though I wanted to - quite the taboo to have any kind of physical contact. I looked at her and smiled.

"*Nanti saya balik*," I managed as a reminder. *I will come back later.* She smiled back and wiped her eyes. We said our goodbyes, then I got on the bus. Avoi promptly put his foot down, and the bus kicked into life and began its drive away, with all of us waving our last goodbye, out of the open bus windows .

Changeover

The return journey to KK was a long one. It also felt like a return to civilization, back to some kind of normality of scenes you would expect from a bustling city. We were to spend one night here at a hostel, catching up with two other teams that had been working elsewhere in Sabah. Upon checking in, it was a joy to see Bro again. We had plenty of down time, so I went to see him in his room and we caught up with stories of what we both got up to. His team were building a brand new longhouse, also in a Rungus community, elsewhere in the Kudat region. It sounded like he also had an amazing time - another village by the sea. I decided to tell him about Sabrinah. Not really knowing how or what to say. *I met a girl* didn't quite cut it. But we knew each other well, and Bro was always someone to see the deeper side of things, and despite being 3 years younger than me, he had the wisdom of someone much older.

"Jeez!" he breathed out, once I finished my tale. "I think you gotta go back, man! You don't really have a choice. Pursue it. You don't know where it will take you. Maybe it won't work out like you think, maybe it will. *Personal legend*, man!" he exclaimed, reminding me of our shared interest in Paulo Coelho's *The Alchemist.*

He was right, and I'm glad he listened and gave me feedback on everything that had been going on my head. It was the validation I needed. Right, that was that. Food beckoned. It was now time to head out to KK's *pasar malam*, or night market, to experience some amazing local food once again, guided by our Malaysian team members once more.

The next morning saw another Malaysian Airlines plane once again being invaded by a sea of blue t-shirts - about sixty of us - to fly from KK to Kuantan, headquarters for Raleigh. All ten teams, the entire expedition, would reconvene at the Kuantan sports complex where I had passed my swimming test seemingly ages ago. It was a great celebration and knees up for all, a night out at the local night club, and up early the next day for our baked beans on toast breakfast. Each team gave a presentation of how their phase went, encouraged to be as creative as possible, either as a performance, a speech, or anything we saw fit. For our Phase One group, we improvised those Rungus gongs with our cooking pots and pans, and gave the audience our traditional Rungus dance to lots of cheers and laughter.

Next came the bit we were all waiting for - what second project we would be in, and with who. When my turn came up, I was called up by Gary, the Expedition Leader. I was to be going to a place called Tasik Bera, on the mainland this time, to help a scientist carry out research on the wetlands there. *Tasik* meant *lake*. Another Malay word for me to bank. This was an area of international significance and importance, situated in the Pahang area of Peninsular Malaysia.

"Proceed to your group over there," instructed Gary, pointing toward where a group had slowly been forming. As I approached, I could see many new faces, and, much to my delight, some familiar ones. Saini was still with me! As was Bella and Minnie. I had already met a few of the others. Our new group leader was a guy called Edgar - not a person I had come across before - who had already spent one phase at Tasik Bera. Each group leader would spend the entire time at their allocated project, unlike us venturers who would change every three weeks. This meant Lorraine would be returning back to the village, albeit with a new team. It made sense to have continuity and maintain some familiarity with each project, so the changeovers ran smoothly. Once our new group had all assembled, Edgar gave his talk.

"OK guys! Welcome to your Phase Two group. It's an awesome project in an awesome location. We have to travel by bus from here, deep into the Pahang region of Malaysia. The bus drops us off at the edge of the rainforest, where we will be heading in to our campsite. The campsite is our base, and it lies on the edge of this massive lake and wetlands. We will be helping two scientists working out there to gather soil samples from the bottom of the lake. They have been studying the area and conducting a lot of research there. It's a very unique place in the world, so we are all lucky to be going there and taking part in this thing."

He went on and explained that this area was home to the *Semelai* people, also known as *Orang Asli*, which in rough translation meant aboriginal people. Although we wouldn't be staying with them, we would be passing by their village areas in the boat. We had to remember to act appropriately and be respectful as we were guests in the area. They were not used to having many guests nearby, especially a group of foreigners. So, we were in for a treat. More jungle, more rainforest, and more tribes of people. And it was only our second project of the expedition.

Tasik Bera

We had gotten used to some jungle both in Sabah and on the peninsular just outside of Kuantan, but as our bus approached the end of its journey to Tasik Bera, this was really something else. Sleeping for most of the journey - I had found a way somehow - I didn't get to see the landscape go by at all. The trees here were different. Much taller, and huge roots coming out of the lower end of the trunk. On automatic now, we got our belongings and headed into the jungle on instruction from Edgar.

It wasn't too far from the dirt track we had come along before we made it to 'scout camp'. This was the main site where we were to stay. This project consisted of making the site, keeping it tidy, performing camp duties, and heading off into the wetlands by small motor boats in rostered groups. The working days would be long, and if it wasn't your turn to head out into the boats, you had long days back at the camp. Our sleeping quarters were again just the bashers that we had to build. From the recent Phase One group here, Edgar had established a large community area under a huge tarp, with three or four long tables used for eating, chilling out, or playing chess or cards. There was an established cooking area, and a toilet 'zone' was a designated area a slight walk away from the camp. No portaloos this time. One of the highlights of the camp area, was the jetty where the motor boats were. It was at the edge of the most beautiful lake which stretched on for miles. Tasik Bera is the largest freshwater wetland in Malaysia, surrounded by absolutely lush jungle. Edgar explained that this jetty was a great hangout area in the evening, watching a sky untouched by light pollution, and made a great place for a night dip.

It wasn't long before we got into routine and took part in the collection of samples for the two Austrian scientists Jacob and Emilia. A couple of local Semelai guys would also be working with us, steering the boats. Each time we went out, it was clear why the days were long: the boats went out on a trip at least an hour away before we got to little channels in between the grasses that grew there, before we started pushing our sample poles down into the water.

The days spent in the camp allowed plenty of time to get to know each other, fill in our journals and play cards. I made a very close Chinese friend there, called Gemma. She was definitely a character, and made the life and soul of the team. She was Chinese Malaysian from Kuala Lumpur, and a friend of Minnie also. We had many an interesting conversation in our time at Tasik Bera, and she quickly discovered about my adventures in Sabah, and all about Sabrinah. She was another Malaysian who could give me a lot of insight into the Asian, or even Malaysian, way of life.

As for our surroundings, it quickly became evident that this was a completely different type of jungle, from the different coloured pitcher plants, to the larger taller trees, to the wildlife crawling, creeping and prowling around. There were elephants known to be further into the jungle, though we didn't see any.

Plenty of monkeys on the treetops too, but most of what we saw was crawling around the campsite. On one day, a bright blue scorpion as big as my hand appeared, scuttling along the ground near some of our bashers. Edgar seemed to know what to do - or maybe he was foolishly brave - as he knelt forward and somehow coaxed it onto the flat of his palm. He then picked it up by it's tail and walked off to let it free away from the camp. This second project was clearly different from the one in the village.

Unfortunately for me, my time here in Tasek Bera was cut short. Into the second week, I woke up feeling slightly under the weather with what I thought was a mild cold, coupled with a headache. I was supposed to go out on the boats that day, but asked to swap shifts and stay back at the camp, since I felt run-down. Our team nurse, Vikki, agreed.

"You do look a bit off colour. Yes, you'd better stay on camp today. Let me take your temperature." She shoved a mercury thermometer under my armpit and hunted her pack for panadol. "37.5. Ok, no problem. I'll check on you later though, I don't like the way you look at the moment."

Feeling drained of energy, I simply nodded in acknowledgment and made my way back to an unoccupied hammock, craving some relaxation. I was grateful for my fellow teammates at the camp, who took on my own duties for the day. Gemma was busying the kitchen area, cleaning the breakfast up and prepping the food for lunch. I could feel smoke waft down from the further side of the camp, where Bella was starting a fire. I must have drifted to sleep briefly - as is so easily done when in a hammock - but I woke up startled and shivering. I felt cold now, for the first time in ages. I pulled out my evening shirt from my bag, long-sleeved to cover up from the mozzies, and put it on over my t-shirt. It felt bizarre to need an extra layer in this heat. My body started to ache, so I wandered over to where Bella was, at least to move about. She had a good fire going, which was no easy feat in a wet and humid jungle.

"Hey, Sam! How are you feeling?" she asked.

"Cold! So cold!" was my reply. I squatted down next to the fire, and held out my hands, grateful for its heat. How odd this must have been, in the heat of the midday sun in the jungle, to be fully clothed and close to a fire, shivering. I turned to Bella once more, but she had gone. I started to ache even more, and went from my squat to just sitting directly on the jungle floor. This is not something you should normally do, given what might be crawling around (usually ants that bite - if you're lucky), but I was beyond caring, and probably didn't even think about it at the time. I heard some voices nearby. Bella returned with Vikki - she had obviously gone to get her after seeing me like this. Vikki thrusted another thermometer under my arm as I shivered. She looked at it, and then at me.

"Bloody hell, let's get him out of here. Now!" She took off my extra layer, and lay me down on a bench, giving me water. Bella had ran straight to the radio, to call in for Mr. Tang, our Lord of the Ringgits, who was on standby to evacuate anyone who needed to be.

I'm not really sure what happened after that. I have memories of being in a car, and the unfortunate act of emptying my stomach by the roadside.. Mr. Tang driving somewhere. Another venturer was in the front seat. I wasn't sure of his name, and was too ill to ask. He looked unwell too. Then, just like that, I found myself in a hospital bed. I must have conked out again in the car. Several nurses surrounded me, bombarding me with questions while a foreign sensation coursed through my arm—an intravenous drip, I presumed. How long had I been here? As I became more coherent, I took in the surroundings. A small hospital room, with one other bed to my side. The other venturer was there, sleeping.

It reminded me of a scene many years ago, when I was 16. A car had run me over on my bicycle, and sped off. I have no memory of the event, and only woke up in a hospital bed not knowing how I had got there. There was a TV in the room back then, blaring news of the outbreak of the first Gulf War. Bush Senior was giving a speech.

"Has the war started, then?" were the first words I uttered, as I suddenly realised my mum was standing at the end of the bed, worried sick.

Now it seemed that history was repeating itself, albeit no TV, no Gulf war, and no head injury from a hit and run incident. So what was wrong with me this time? As I sat up, a voice came from the end of the bed. Not my mother's this time.

"Lay down, Hyman! You are not well. We are running some tests on your blood, you obviously have a fever of some kind and we need to rule out Malaria and Dengue," stated a spindly looking Doctor dressed in white overalls. He even had a stethoscope around his neck. He looked very stern, not someone to mess with.

"I am Dr. Patel. Just get some rest. Drink. Don't worry about food just yet if you can't keep it down. The nurses will get you something if you need, ok, Hyman?" He obviously took my surname as my first name, but I had no energy to correct him. Hyman it was. I lay back down and soon fell asleep.

I awoke again from the nurses prodding me. Taking more blood, checking my drip and changing it. Asking me if I had passed water, or had any bowel movements. I shook my head. Wow... that hurt. Next time I will just say no. As I looked toward the end of the bed, this time Nick was there.

"Alright, Sam? I see you are a bit under the weather. Same with Les, next to you. Different camp but same symptoms." He shrugged his shoulders. "I guess the doctor will get to the bottom of it. Anyway, you're in the right place. Nice private hospital, thanks to the Raleigh Insurance. I don't know how much longer you have to stay, but best to take each day as it comes. Here, take this." He threw a book on to the end of my bed. "Excellent read, that. Give you something to do. I'll be back to visit when I can!"

And with that, he turned, and left. I sat up and picked up the book. Typical of Nick, a book about the army. Bravo Two Zero by Andy McNab, a book that had recently come out and was climbing the book charts. I was grateful for it though, since it would give me something to do in this windowless room.

Several times each day, the nurses would wake me for food, drink, and questions about my bowel movements. The only times I could get out of bed was to go to the toilet, dragging my drip stand each time. Unfortunately the trip from my bed to the toilet didn't pass any windows. I craved a view of the outdoors, and forgot what it was like.

Once a day, was a visit from my stern-faced balding Doctor.

"How are you today, Hyman?" followed by, "I'm sorry, you can't leave yet. Your platelet levels are really low and we need to wait until they regenerate to a safe level.

Apparently I did not have Malaria or Dengue, or any other

recognisable fever. It was the Doctor's turn to shrug.

"Sometimes we can catch something that we know nothing about. You were in the jungle. It could be anything. But while your symptoms are improving, your platelets are not enough yet."

It wasn't that encouraging to hear that he had no idea what it was. Maybe I should be grateful that he ruled out those other two diseases though. Each day came with a prayer of mine. A prayer that just wished the Doctor would say my platelet level had reached the required level. I sank into despair each time he said no.

A grueling, desperate ten whole days later, the Doctor finally gave me the green light to leave. I had finished Brave Two Zero a couple of days ago and was starting to go crazy. Les had gone after five days, so it was just me in these four walls of no windows. As Mr. Tang came up to collect me from the ward and get me officially discharged, I yearned for the first window I could feast my eyes upon. And there it was, after walking down one of the corridors. I stopped and stared outside. The world! I was so happy to see it. Mr. Tang drove me back to headquarters for another day, before the long drive towards Tasik Bera. I felt different, really different. Full of energy as if I had had a complete overhaul. Not just recovered but better than I ever was. It was a strange feeling. As Mr. Tang dropped me off near the camp, I walked in with my belongings once more to see my fellow team, for the first time in what felt like ages.

"Wow, look at you! What happened? You look great!" Vikki said as she embraced me on my return.

"I have no idea, but I feel really good now. Much better, thanks." Similar responses from my other teammates. It felt great to be back. I was lucky to see out the last few days of the Tasik Bera phase two project, especially with a renewed sense of energy and vigour.

I never found out what that bug was that got me so ill, but it felt like it killed off the old me and gave me a rebirth, just in time for what was to be the toughest phase yet.

Leeches & Prayer

Our second changeover time came with the usual reunions, celebrations, a night out in Kuantan again, and the showcases of our projects. I was keen to hear from the Phase Two bridge project, to get any news about the bridge and the everyone in the village. Lorraine said it was all going well, and everything was on target. It was all good news, although it only gave me more feelings of impatience to get back there.

My next project was soon announced, as was my new team. We had two team leaders this time - Keith and Tom. They stood there in front of our newly assembled group, hands on hips and legs astride.

"Oh jeez. Looks like we got proper action men now!" A voice came from behind me. "Hiya, mate, my name's Simon. I'm from Castleford." His strong Yorkshire accent gave him away somewhat, it had a Castleford twang to it. I introduced myself, and then we turned back to our two action men at the front, who were about to speak.

"Congratulations! You've made it into the best team for your last Phase Three project. Rainforest trekking. It ain't easy!" said Keith, the taller of the two. They looked similar, shaved heads, well built and full of bravado. This was definitely going to be an interesting group!

"Nope! It ain't easy. I know you've all been in the jungle already. Maybe seen a few things. But this is something else. It will be at least a two week trek, and include hiking up Gunung Tahan," Tom added, hands still firm on the hips.

"Gunung Tahan means Mount Endurance in English, it's the highest point on Peninsular Malaysia. We've managed it twice already with Phase One and Phase Two groups, but not everyone in those teams could climb it. Some even had to be evacuated, as you may have heard," Keith warned.

This part was true. Three venturers had left the expedition and got the next flight home. They were all from the jungle trekking phases, led by Keith and Tom. They complained it wasn't what they thought the expedition would be about. Which was odd, since that is exactly what the expedition was about. A couple of others had to return to headquarters due to illness or injury too. Not a great advert for a project.

"But, things have got easier," Keith continued, "we got things a bit wrong on the first phase. We learned more doing it a second time. You guys are luckier. We know we don't need to pack tins of food - they are too heavy. Flat packed food works better. Anyway, it's things like that which will help the whole trek run smoother, and we will have a better chance of getting the entire group through the trek from start to finish. We couldn't manage it with the other two groups due to injuries and accidents. Based on that, the first few days once we get to the start point, is to undergo some specific safety training and techniques. For now, we will leave you to gather your things and we will meet up at the bus point. Don't worry too much about sorting out what you need to carry for the trek, we can do that later."

That left us time to chill for a short while longer, and get to know each other in our new team. At this point, I was pretty saturated though, so I went off and hung out with Seb and Bro. Seb was now off to Sabah, for his turn in a village somewhere, and Bro was in a trekking group, also in the National Park albeit from a different start point. The previous Phases had set the route, and the Orang Asli guides we were hiring already knew of a route through.

After yet another long journey to the start point, on the edge of the National Park Taman Negara, we used a small hut to stay in whilst Tom and Keith ran us through some protocols and methods which would come in handy during the trek. The difference with this project was that each time we set up camp, it was for one night only. We had to keep moving through the rainforest, making sure we left nothing behind as we went. Setting up a temporary one-night camp still involved erecting our bashers in between suitably spaced trees, finding a place away from camp for a toilet area, and positioning the all important radio mast to ensure a signal for calling in each day.

During the day, Tom and Keith made sure that we could build effective bashers quickly - since the time we had to erect a camp was narrow, and it would come after trekking throughout the day. We would only trek in the day time, as it would be far too dangerous at night. We also had to watch out for falling trees. This could happen at any time, without warning. And the trees, we were warned, could be the largest we have ever seen. Streams could become raging torrents in minutes, given the way the rain fell and the ground collected and funneled the water. Wildlife? Expect anything. This was proper rainforest with all the added extras: not just monkeys and spiders this time.

Elephants, tigers, leopards, wild boars, and even the Sumatran rhinoceros lived in this massive area of jungle.

"You'd better hope not to see any elephants though!" Keith said, "although it would be amazing in theory, our guides said these animals will charge when they see humans. With any luck, we will hear them from a distance only."

Another aspect we had to sort out was who would be carrying what, in terms of what supplies and equipment we would need for the entire trek. Enough food for fifteen people for two weeks, a water filter, a barrel, a radio and its equipment, and medical supplies. This was on top of our own belongings such as stretchers, nets and tarps for our bashers, dry and wet sets of clothes, sandals for when we finished a day's trek (very important to take off those boots after walking for a day in the jungle), water bottle, mess tins, torch, and water proof canoe bags to keep everything dry. Thanks to my large army backpack, I was designated to carry the barrel inside my bag, and fit everything else into it. It turned out the barrel was useful, to hold the filtered water once we pumped it from whatever water source we could find each day.

Once we started, it soon became apparent just how different and grueling things were. The trails were hard, and sometimes needed hacking through with a machete. Other times we were either climbing up or sliding down very steep inclines. The ground itself was never flat, constantly slippy and had roots all over the place. Natural instinct was to grab hold of a branch upon slipping: bad idea. Many trees had very thick black needles sticking out, which were incredibly painful. The physical effort really took its toll as each day passed, and brought out a lot of emotion in some of the team members. It was a difficult task to encourage some members in tears who said they couldn't go on. We had no choice but to continue. It wasn't a place you could simply split up and leave.

If it wasn't the exhaustion that got you, it might have been the leeches. They were everywhere, and you wouldn't know if you had any hanging off you. Once they found a way to attach itself to your body - and they always found a way in - their bite releases a naturally occurring anesthetic that numbs the area. You only find out about it by looking. Maybe you would wake up in the morning in your basher, to find blood stains on your sleeping bag liner. For me, I just focused on the fact that it was an old traditional method in ridding yourself of toxins. At least that's what I told myself to feel better. Other team members would think of vindictive ways of killing them, after collecting the leeches that they found on their bodies.

The climb up Mount Tahan was incredible. On day 5 we reached base camp, where we would set down for the evening, and ready ourselves for the five hour hike to the summit of 2,187 metres. That meant a 10 hour round trip, which had to be done during daylight. It was reported to be one of the toughest treks in Peninsular Malaysia. Temperatures at the summit were around 4C, so staying up there in our gear wasn't an option. It was indeed an incredible climb, with the trees notably shrinking the higher we climbed. Now and again there would be a break in the trees which offered an amazing view of the rainforest we had trekked through over the last few days. It was incredible, we were truly in the middle of nowhere! Endless rolling hills of green right up to the horizon. We could feel the temperature drop considerably the higher we climbed - which of course made sense - but it felt odd after sweating under the jungle canopy for over a week.

Finally reaching the summit, I came across something very unexpected. A large perspex case with a signing-in book inside. After a lot of cheers and embraces, we signed the visitor book, and proudly made our decent. On one hand it was a shame that we couldn't spend longer at the top, but on the other hand it was cold, and standing still in sweaty clothes was not going to end well. Besides we had to get back to camp before dark.

As we neared the camp, the heavens opened. And when they open in the rainforest, they really open. What struck me was the sheer noise of the rain. We had to shout to communicate. Coming down from the mountain became much harder and at a slower pace. Needless to say we were drenched through and exhausted by the time we reached our camp. I sat up on my basher next to Simon, shivering together like a couple of erratic string puppets. All social boundaries were excused between us - we were too tired to change and just cuddled each other for warmth. The camp site was relatively high up altitude wise, and now that we had stopped trekking the cold and damp really set in. Making a fire was also out of the question, there would be no dry wood anywhere and our firelighters had no chance. After a very cold meal and a reluctant change into something relatively dry - those canoe bags really were excellent - we took shelter in our bashers, under our tarps, very grateful in the knowledge that we had become experienced basher builders who could now build shelters to withhold a storm such as this.

After a few more days of trekking, we knew we had made good progress: Tom declared that the day had finally arrived where we could rest – no more sweaty trekking with heavy loads sinking our heels into the jungle floor. He said there was a real beauty spot half an hour away from the camp that we had made, a great place to chill out. And why not? We felt we could afford a bit of pleasure time, to nurse the aches and pains that we all had. Everyone was looking forward to this, with the promise of a break in the tree lines where the sun would get through.

"It's a great place Keith and I discovered on the last trip through, with a place to dip into the river," Tom explained, "We may as well make the most of it – it's the only rest we're going to get: our destination Kuala Koh is still at least five days trek away, weather permitting, and we can't afford to be late."

Leaving the main bulk of our packs at the camp, we headed swiftly out. The general mood of the group had perked up noticeably; after all, we worked hard to be ahead of schedule so we could have a day just like this. Besides, it was such a luxury to be walking without 20kg on your back.

Sure enough, when we arrived the scene was as we were promised: an idyllic beauty spot. We were by the edge of a wide river surrounded by lush dense rainforest on either side. And as promised, the sun was allowed to shine through here, which brought an amazing change in feeling after rummaging around in the dark. In some parts the river meandered slowly around huge rocks randomly dotted around. The rocks were like huge stepping stones inviting you to cross over to the other side. The large flat surfaces of each boulder and rock, provided many places for sunbathing – even with my pale complexion I too had missed such glorious sunshine.

Much of the group immediately went to find their spot, either singularly or in small groups. The towels were out and it was suddenly like a mini tourist zone, albeit only fifteen of us. But here we were in the middle of the dense rainforest of Peninsular Malaysia, in a place rarely visited by human beings, if at all.

"Don't stray too far, make sure you stay in sight of the group"

Tom bellowed, health and safety always on his mind. I looked around for a spot to myself. I wandered upstream, hopping from rock to boulder, to find a place to chill and gather my thoughts.

Comfortably perched on the edge of a cluster of rocks in the middle of the river, my mind drifted into nothingness for some time, mesmerized by the flowing sound of the water. I allowed myself to be completely absorbed by the power of nature around me. Just out of earshot of the rest of the group, all I could hear was the rushing of the river. I started to think about what had happened to me in this amazing country. Sabrinah. The village. Picturing myself there once more. Hopefully I would get back there after this expedition in two weeks time. But two weeks was an eternity in the rainforest. We were in this wet green world, not having seen any sign of civilisation for days. I wondered whether I would be accepted back into the village again now that the bridge project was over, being a lone traveler, returning this time not to build a bridge, but to follow through a gut instinct to be with a girl I hardly knew. A girl who spoke a language I couldn't yet understand, from a culture so different from my own. My logical side stepped in, as it often did, and told me how ridiculous and laughable this was. But deep down I knew it was just something I had to do. I was being pulled like a magnet whether I liked it or not. I had to go with the flow, surely.

Taking this literally, I took a deep breath and lowered myself into the inviting sway of the water, pushing all my thoughts away, emptying my mind once more. The water came up to my chest and was beautifully cooling. It was invigorating, hypnotic almost. I felt like a child let loose in a private paddling pool. I lay back and looked up at the sky, propelling myself about with my feet. The current became a gentle swell easing me in different directions.

Simon happened to be stood on a rock a few yards away, looking at me enjoying myself in my private moment. He said something to me, but I couldn't make out what it was; I was just lying on my back, having fun, hypnotised by the rocking of the water around me. As my body drifted along, the pull of the river gradually became stronger and more directed. I laughed at the way I was being bounced about, bobbing in the water.

Then I realised. *Hang on, I can't actually stop this.* I turned onto my front and tried to feebly wade out of the current to grab a stationary rock. No chance. A second later and the current became stronger. I was being taken down a section of the river. Simon's expression had changed, as had mine. *Bloody hell!* Now what do I do?! I searched ahead, in the direction I was being taken, to see if there was anything else I could grab onto. Heading toward some rocks, I reached out to hold on for dear life, but the rocks were too slippery and the current too strong. They quickly passed me by. The rushing sound became louder and louder. Then I saw the real danger. I was headed towards a section of the river where the water turned white, into a funnel shape that plunged strongly over an edge. I could not see beyond that. I was being turned around, spinning, everything becoming a blur, hard to focus on anything. The current threw my body against a wooden surface which took all the wind out of me. My arms instinctively wrapped around this wooden thing - a stationary trunk lying horizontal in the water. The trunk wasn't moving, it was wedged in, right where the water was funneling white and fast. I felt safe for a split second – my body had a grip and I had stopped short of that edge.

But no. How wrong I was. My whole body was still submerged in the strong pull of the river – only my head and one arm was above the surface. My hands started to slip. I tightened my grip and hugged the trunk for dear life. If all those tree hugging groups could see me now. *This* is how you do it. I turned and looked towards the edge of the water. There was a terrifying drop into a plunge pool. I knew if I let go, that would be the end of me. I would not be coming out of the water again, and besides, my body would be smashed against the sharp rocks below. Everything was happening so quickly now and thoughts flashed past. *Nature*, I thought. It's a killer. *Is this it? Is this how I go?* My body started to give way. I was gripping so hard but my arms started to shake with fatigue. I could see no way out of this mess. What a stupid idiot I was to end up like this – nobody's fault but mine. Any second now and I knew I would have to let go and give up the battle. I was facing death full on and I became terrified that I would have to accept it in this way. My will to hold on started to falter.

Then I heard a voice. I didn't know where it came from in all my panic and confusion, but it cut through the rush of the water.

"Just pull yourself *up* out of the water," the voice said.

I got it. Right – I was struggling against the current when I just needed to lift myself up and out of the water onto the trunk itself. Less resistance that way! I did what the voice said. It took tremendous effort but it beat just trying to pull against the current. Finally, I pulled my body onto the trunk that I was clinging onto so hard. I rolled onto my back, feeling that the trunk was wedged against a flat rock surface. I was out of the water, at last, finally, physically drained. No energy to keep my eyes open, my whole body numb. I was in some kind of shock for sure.

"Are you alright?! Bloody Hell!" The same voice from earlier.

I was away from death. I survived. I met death and survived. So that's what looking at death feels like. My eyes slowly opened, searching for the voice.

"I saw you get into trouble. You were nearly a gonner, then!!" It was Simon. He had seen me all this time, and hopped over to some nearby rocks to the trunk. Slowly, I lifted myself up to face him. I couldn't say much – I was still in shock, my heart pounding so hard it wanted to burst out of my chest.

"Thanks, Si. Thanks." It was all I could manage.

I looked down and noticed my chest was battered and bleeding – the trunk I was thrown against was rough, like sand paper and my body had been dragged along it. Because of the adrenaline I hadn't felt a thing. Simon walked back, and I slowly made my own way across the rocks towards the rest of the group, completely dazed and disconnected to everything and everyone. I was in a trance. I passed Tom, who looked at me and my scraped chest unforgivingly.

"I told you not to go too far!" he tutted, having no idea what I had just been through, since he and the rest of the group were well out of earshot and sight of where I had been.

I carried on walking and found a spot to myself once more, though this time not so far from the group. Thoughts and images of what just happened raced through my head, as I stood there trying to process it all. For the first time, I had been so close to death that I felt it grip me and pull me in just as the current did. It was real. If I had died there and then, I certainly wouldn't have gone quietly like an obedient little boy. I wasn't ready. I had more to do, more to see. It just wasn't my time yet. That moment, that horrifying realization of how close I had come to death, has remained etched in my memory to this very day. And along with it, an immense gratitude towards Simon, the person who saved my life. He was an effortless hero, his simple words of encouragement—"Climb up out of the river"—altering the course of my fate. Without his timely intervention, I wouldn't have mustered the strength to do it myself, and that would have been the end of my story.

Some years later I bumped into Simon in Leeds City Centre. I thanked him again, though I don't think he ever realised how essential his being there at those rocks was. "Ah, yeah! I remember that. That was crazy. No worries!"

But back in the jungle, my mind was racing and playing those recent images again and again. To regain my composure, I inhaled deeply, attempting to steady my trembling body. It dawned on me that gratitude was owed not only to Simon, but to something beyond my understanding. Overwhelmed with emotion, I instinctively sank to my knees, closing my eyes and lowering my head. I spoke to anything or anyone that was listening. *Thank you.*

The Final Climb

After another grueling week of trekking, we finally made it to Kuala Koh, our destination. It was an exhilarating feeling to get there. For some, it was not a moment too soon – tears had been shed many a time during the last fourteen days, because some of the team did not feel comfortable at all to be so long in that dark rainforest.

For me, I managed to find the deepest sleep I ever had. The constant noise of the jungle at night had become a lullaby for me. And in the years to come it would be a noise I would still never forget, and often yearn for. Each phase of the expedition gave me something different. This last one was much more of a personal journey; a meditative journey of self-discovery. A hard physical demand on my entire body.

Now at a small village on the edge of this pristine rainforest, we had a couple of days before making the journey back to Kuantan. The rest, and the opportunity to eat 'normal' food we hadn't had for what seemed like an age, was very welcomed!

Once in Kuantan for the third time, we quickly regrouped to fly out to Sabah for what would be the final task of the expedition: to climb Mount Kinabalu. Rather than a project, it was presented as a challenge – the sort of thing we would do to raise money, only this time the challenge itself was on a much more grander scale. Reaching a height of 4095 metres, Mount Kinabalu is a major landmark in Sabah, and even features on the state flag. I didn't know much about the mountain, but I was told that it was a very sacred place to the indigenous people here. It's name came from the local Kadazan people, who called it *Aki Nabalu*. Although there were many stories surrounding it, the common feature that threads through all of them was that it was considered a resting place of the spirits of their ancestors. It reminded me of the more famous Uluru in Australia, which was regarded in a similar way.

As we sat in the bus winding up to the park entrance, the team had mixed emotions. By this stage, having spent ten weeks on the expedition, we were ready to do anything. At the same time, there was a lot of exhaustion too. This was a larger group now, and Bro was in my team. As always, we exchanged stories of our different experiences so far. Having been through such an arduous trek which ended only two days ago, this climb coming up seemed like an extension of that. It was amazing to hear that he had been in Endau Rompin, a protected area of primary rainforest in Pahang. He had helped develop a salt lick there with his team, in conjunction with the National Park of Malaysia. We also caught up about news of Seb, and what he had got up to. Neither of us has seen much of him throughout the expedition, except for a couple of days catch up on the change-overs in Kuantan. Seb climbed Mount Kinabalu early on in the expedition, and had said that the weather had turned on them - they got very wet and cold, but still made it to the peak. He was buzzing after that climb despite what he described as a nightmare of a challenge.

Once the bus arrived at the park entrance, we were afforded another chance of rest. We stayed overnight in the small cabins at the park base, which was at an altitude of just over 1000m. We could feel a notable chill in the air, but this slight drop in temperature was very welcome, and felt strange after being in the tropics.

The next morning, we donned our packs and started the climb. It was a truly beautiful part of the world that seemed to change every few hundred metres. Everything that grew, gradually got shorter and shorter the higher we reached. The climb at this stage seemed endless, the views amazing. Occasionally I would get a view of the mountain's peak looming ahead. So far the weather was being kind, I hoped it would stay that way - it meant clear views. It would be very disappointing to come all this way to be surrounded by damp fog. Marching on, our group became separated due to the varying pace that we each had. Some needed longer rests along the way. For long stretches of the climb, I didn't see many people in our group.

A few hours later I got to Laban Rata, a camp at 3200m. The trees became more and more sparse here, and almost bonsai like in size. Most of the terrain now was just rock. It was this place where the whole climb caught up with me - I could stop and take everything in. The cold set in quickly - made worse by my sweaty clothes from the climb. All that damp clothing was something I knew I had to get out of quickly, now that I wasn't moving around so much. Some of my team had arrived before me and had already checked in to the dorm hut, changed into their dry set of clothes and headed a couple of hundred metres away to another building, where food was being served. As I made the last few steps towards the dorms, Karl came out with a grin on his face.

"Milo." he exclaimed. "They have milo here. At 3000 metres up. Milo! Get changed, my friend, and join me for a hot one!" He scuttled off out of the dorm hut and headed straight for the restaurant. I watched him hop down, like a child looking for sweets. I could understand it though; by now I was thirsting for one too. The backdrop to Karl wandering down the rocky path was crazy. A green valley down below, miles away. The occasional cloud floating in, below us. It reminded me of the kind of views you get looking out of a aeroplane window. To the right, the towering rocky mass which made up the rest of the peak we needed to climb the next morning. It was an odd feeling to know, that this high up, there was still more mountain to climb!

I changed out of my wet clothes, and hung them up on the line outside the room. I suddenly realised that doing even simple tasks like this took so much effort with the thinner oxygen. The quick transition of getting this high made the climb that much harder – and at 3000 metres, altitude sickness could still be a risk. It took a great effort for me to get out of my room and head down to the restaurant, just a short walk away. That short walk became increasingly hard to do, but the thought of a hot milo kept me going. I thought about the oddness of having a restaurant so high up here. This was made possible by the local Kadazan climbers whose job it was to carry supplies up everyday. In addition to that, they would bring down the restaurant waste on the return journey. It was astounding to see these individuals effortlessly hop from rock to rock, step to step, whilst carrying a massive load on their back. I recalled seeing one or two of them coming down, as I climbed up. Now I understood what it was all for.

Stepping into the restaurant, I headed straight for the counter to order. Fried noodles and a hot milo. I couldn't believe I was able to order such things. I sat with Karl, Bro, and a few others whilst we took it all in. The view from our table was stunning, looking out of the huge window beside us. Again, rolling mist and clouds would come and go, allowing glimpses of parts of the mountain, and valleys down below. We sat for a long time, eating and resting. There was still a few hours of sunlight, but we knew once it got dark it was time to huddle up in the dorms and try to keep warm. Seb had warned us that at this height, we should forget any idea of getting sleep. The changes in air made that extremely hard to do. He was right. After getting back to the bunk beds in the dorm, we all just lay there and tossed and turned hopelessly, just trying to breathe, knowing that we should get ready for the wake up call at 2AM to start the climb to the summit, in the dark.

The advantage of having this dorm at 3000m was that we could leave our packs there. This last 1000m of climbing would be the hardest, and the knowledge that we only had to carry the bare essentials - torch, water and a whistle -was most welcome.

Starting this part of the climb was entirely different - it was pitch black, and very cold. We spoke in hushed voices, partly to be quiet for others at this early hour, and partly because it was such an effort to speak. I was glad that I couldn't see the trail in front of me now, I didn't want to know how much further I had to go. I was happy that I could still move one foot in front of the other, and keep going despite the altitude.

Unfortunately for Karl this high altitude became all too much. He couldn't make the last part of the climb to the summit, as that night altitude sickness had set in. Being an intrepid climber, it must have been hard for him to have had to sit there and wait for his team to climb up and then return – but he knew it would be far too dangerous to continue. We didn't speak too much about this at the time - it was all too disappointing for him. Actually it wasn't until ten years later I finally met up with him in the UK for the first time since the expedition. It was great to finally track him down via Facebook, and see him again after such a long time. I was staying with my Aunt in the picturesque village of Portinscale near Keswick. He wasn't too far away, so he set out to meet me in the village pub. It was a great reunion of two friends that had not spoken a word to each other since 1997. It was in 2007, we spoke about that last climb which had ended the expedition.

"I was gutted," Karl reflected, "but it was my own fault. From the start of the climb I just pumped all the way up to Laban Rata without stopping. I was exhausted and there was no way I could finish the climb. And maybe too much Milo? I've never felt that sick before!"

As I pressed on towards the summit, the terrain transformed into a lunar-like landscape, with craters, gullies, and eerie silhouettes of peaks shaping the darkness. The simple act of putting one foot in front of the other, a skill acquired in our early years, now became an arduous task. Approaching 4000 metres, everything became much more of an effort and my breathing became more and more laboured. As I made frequent stops to catch my breath, I reflected how sacred this place was. My mind was in a strange dream-like state, and I could hear myself asking permission to continue, that I would be respectful of the mountain as I sought to walk upon it. Standing still for too long, I thought I might join the departed – the cold set in quick, so I marched on, determined not to stop again until I reached the top.

Our group had once again scattered, each member grappling with their own pace and personal struggles. Behind me, flickering torchlights bobbed in the distance, gradually receding until they nearly vanished. Most of us were inexperienced climbers, and our lack of cohesion at this final stage was evidence of that. It was at times unnerving to be alone in the dark. I could see at least one figure ahead of me, though, heading in the same direction to reach the top. I had no idea who it was – I had lost track of any anyone else, and being so dark it was easy to be out of range of sight. The howling wind whipping up around me prevented any calling out, which was just as well because I had no energy to speak by now. Still, keeping to the vague trail which occasionally had ropes to assist the steep parts of the climb, I knew I was relatively safe. Straying from these life lines at this point and at this altitude would be life threatening. In this vast darkness devoid of life, losing sight of the path meant perilous ledges lay in wait. Retracing one's steps would be next to impossible. Even in daylight, people had lost their lives albeit in more treacherous conditions than this day.

Once, two young British teenagers had strayed from the ropes on the way down after sunrise. They clambered down the trail to meet their parents who were waiting for them at Laban Rata. With a cruel twist of fate, fog had quickly set in taking away any visibility over a couple of metres. They never made it back to Laban Rata to tell their parents they made it to the summit. It took days for the mountain rescue team to find them. According to the local paper, the rescue team could hear the echoing cries for help, but the unforgiving gales threw their pleas across the entire mountain top, making it impossible to locate them. Sadly, after three sleepless nights, the mountain rangers and guides carried down the two bodies in coffins.

For my climb, the weather was still being relatively kind, as biting as it was. I looked up ahead into the darkness, and by a dancing spot of light I could still see that figure ahead of me. Whoever it was, there was no way to catch up with them. It was like a demon teasing me to my death, beckoning to follow in the darkness. To keep myself going in this last stage, I fixated on catching up to whoever it was. Was it my imagination? Shadows danced around as my head torch flickered about. I turned round to sense if anyone was behind me. Not a soul. My mind was faltering, I had more and more moments where things stopped making sense. My brain slowed down again, exhausted. Then I came back to reality, and realised I was stood motionless in the dark, approaching near 4000m. And I remembered to press on.

The ground became very steep once more. I could make out that the figure ahead had stopped. I climbed on, then saw that the rocky ground levelled out slightly. Surely this was it? Had I reached the end of the climb, got to the peak? My head torch searched for the figure, and found it's face which lit up like the moon. Beaming from ear to ear was Bro's face, squinting by the light of my torch. An avid climber himself, he had pumped up the mountain full speed, hardly batting an eyelid. "This is it! We've done it!" he cried. Sure enough, next to him was the plaque embedded in the rock, shining gold bouncing the light from our torches, reading "LOWES PEAK 4096m". We cheered like crazy, lifting each other up and jumping about like mad hyenas. What a journey we made together, all the way from Leeds.

I cannot accurately describe the exhilaration, the relief and the triumph that we felt at that moment. But perhaps you might have heard it; our cheers and screams of success must have been heard by most of Sabah. Here we were, on the roof of Borneo!

Jumping up and down in the dark, we were soon joined by Saini. He hadn't been far behind me, and I must have missed sighting him in my many turns around. So our private two-man party became three, and the celebration continued in the darkness. As time went on, cheers of triumph would continue as other team members finally reached the summit in turn.

Those of us that had arrived earlier were starting to feel the cold, since we had stopped hiking. We had to concentrate on keeping warm, waiting for the sun to make its appearance. The hues of the morning sky was like nothing else I have ever seen. We were lucky because the weather was perfectly clear, and it made a great opportunity for photos. As the sun slowly rose, I finished a full roll of film. Looking behind me, I saw that the mountain peak made a triangular shadow in the western sky. It was absolutely magical.

The peak I was standing on could be seen all over Sabah, even from as far as Sabrinah's village to the north. I looked out in that direction. This sunrise marked the end of the expedition, and there couldn't have been a better way to end it. Breathing deeply, taking in as much of the fresh but thin oxygen as I could, I knew it wouldn't be long now before I would make my way back to Sabrinah's village, alone.

Endings & Beginnings

The expedition had come to its grand finale. Every group had finished in various parts of Malaysia, each venturer having their own amazing, unique experience. Each group did a final showcase, with a final slideshow from the expedition photographer. It really fired home just what an amazing project this was for all of us.

It was an odd feeling that hit us all, the way this moment had crept up suddenly. We had made very close friendships – would we see each other again? Tears and hugs everywhere, between Malaysian venturers and those from the UK in particular. Promises were made to fly over and see each other again, despite being on the other side of the world. The goodbye event we had in Leeds in front of the civic hall only three months earlier couldn't have been more different. Back then I just wanted to get on the plane and go, not interested in the emotional farewells. I had changed. It is very hard to describe these short 10 weeks we had together. Maybe it came at just the right time in our lives, most of us being in our late teens to early twenties. Maybe it was something to do with the diversity of the group – students, police officers, paramedics, doctors, unemployed, shop assistants, accountants, office workers, builders, and café vendors. Perhaps for some, not knowing that we would ever see each other again was a hard pill to swallow. There was a determination to keep our promises to meet up in the future, somehow, somewhere.

I am glad to say that for many, that promise was kept. Over the years to come, UK venturers found their way back to KL, and then even on to some of the remote project sites they worked on. Ant brought his wife back to the village to show the bridge he had built years ago. Another venturer from a different phase, Kate, came back to Sabah with her husband and son to show what she had done, and meet her old friends too. A few Malaysian venturers came over to Leeds to seek out who was still around. My good friends Minnie and Gemma came over too. Our expedition has since had various anniversary parties, 5, 10 and 20 years. One Malaysian venturer who could only speak basic English at the time, had since gone on to Newcastle University, graduated in Law, and became a very successful lawyer. Somehow we ended up finding each other again: we both ended up in Brunei only 10 minutes away from each other. I had met up with him there in a speakeasy bar, over 20 years since I had seen him on the expedition itself. By this time, he was fluent in English, and mastered his snooker skills to the point of thrashing me at the table, which doesn't happen often!

Every person I have seen since Expedition 97G has said the same. We were part of something special.

Back in Kuantan, as the final curtain of the expedition came down in the form of a presentation by senior staff, we all started to head back to our dorms and gather our things. Plans had been made – many would go on to travel the rest of South East Asia in small groups of friends they had made from the expedition, not ready to face going home, and in pursuit of more adventure.

Some sadly had no choice, and had to get back to the UK for family or employment reasons. Most of the Malaysians had to return to KL where they lived, to restart their lives too, and go back to their jobs. I said my goodbyes to Seb and Bro, who were headed on a backpacking adventure to Thailand. I would have gone with them, but the three of us knew there was only one place I had to go. It didn't need much explaining.

Whilst everyone seemed to have traveling companions, I was to be on my own for the first time, with a seemingly impossible task: to somehow find my way back to where Sabrinah's village was, without the help of expedition buses or trip organisers. I knew the name of the village, but no one in the towns or cities ever heard of that name, let alone the name of the tribe of people that lived there.

I sat and waited. Once the sports complex almost emptied out, I put on my heavy backpack, which contained everything I had left from a 10 week jungle expedition, and headed to the nearest bus stop.

There & Back Again

My first port of call was to head to the opposite side of Peninsular Malaysia, and get to the main Bus Station in Kuala Lumpur known as KL Sentral. I had arranged to meet Saini there. He thought it would be a good idea for me to stay in his apartment for a few days in KL, before heading back to Sabah.

It was a long and lonely bus ride back to KL, but thankfully it stopped right near the station I was looking for. KL Sentral Bus Station was an unremarkable, dreary grey building devoid of any aesthetic appeal. People were everywhere, it seemed chaotic. The air was thick with pollution and a medley of odors emanating from the food stalls, intensified by the constant city heat. Clusters of fixed blue plastic chairs were dotted around, all of which seemed to be occupied by people. Many passengers were bedded down for a lengthy stay, in any nook or cranny where they had found it possible to lie down and sleep. A lot of people did this with a newspaper spread across their face in a feeble attempt to block out the chaos around them. This was a perfect place to die, I mused, no one would know for ages.

It was a large terminal, so Saini had told me to find the only 'Dunkin Donuts' stall and wait for him there. He didn't give a time, but he knew I would be arriving early evening. I found the

Donuts stall, but passed on getting any since the atmosphere was not exactly the most conducive for eating. I found some floor space - not a place you would want to park up, but I had little choice, the seats were all taken. At least I had my backpack to place down and lie half of my body on. Time seemed to slip away as I felt like a character in a time-lapse film, lying there, observing the people around me. Saini was nowhere to be found, and with no means of contacting him, I was left with the choice of either continuing to wait or venturing onward by myself. Opting to wait a little longer, I eventually drifted off to sleep, my arms wrapped protectively around my bag.

I came to, as I felt someone continually tap me on my shoulder. It was Saini hovering over me.

"Sam! I am so sorry, so sorry! I was delayed getting to KL. Are you OK?"

I told him I was fine, just a bit hungry. I wondered how long it had been. As Saini led my dazed body back outside the terminal, I saw by the big clock that it was 3AM. It was surprising to see that the activity in the terminal was just as chaotic and alive at this late hour too. Finally Saini and I got back to his apartment after a short taxi ride, and I collapsed on his sofa.

The next day we discussed and reminisced about the mad three months we just had. Saini didn't have much time to offer, since he was due back to work the next day.

"I'll be serving on a flight tomorrow, so I'll need to rest. But in the meantime, take a look at this - I will show you how to get to Singapore and back, before you take your own flight back to Sabah." He started to write out some notes for me.

His information was extremely helpful - I didn't have what would have been the most useful thing at the time, like a Lonely

Planet guide to the area. After he explained everything, getting the bus from KL to Singapore and back for a visa run seemed very straight forward, even for me. I was to take the night bus and sleep the 6 hour southbound journey. My flight from KL to KK in Sabah was the next day, so I had to get back from Singapore straight away. There and back again. I just assumed that would be easy.

Later that evening Saini took me to the bus station for Singapore, and this was to be our final goodbye - an emotional one, since we didn't know when we would see each other again. He would be up in the air with Malaysian Airlines as cabin crew, and I would be heading for Sabah for who knows how long. We had been through a lot together throughout the expedition, and had built a good friendship. Saini was also the last expedition member to say farewell to, I would truly be on my own from here on in. I thanked him for everything he had done, for our friendship, and made a pledge to see him again sometime in the future.

As I stepped onto the bus, I already started to miss his sense of humour and that laugh of his. I found my seat near the back of the bus, and got comfortable. This 'business class' bus was like no other I had experienced. The seats were comfy red leather and very spacious. It could recline far back without disturbing other passengers. I took a quick look around, and realised the bus was fairly full, to my surprise, for a mid week night bus. Not so interested in the scenery during the night, I got my head down and slept surprisingly well for the majority of the journey.

I awoke as I felt the bus come to a halt. Looking outside, I realised we had arrived at the Malaysian-Singapore border, and needed to get out and have our passports stamped. Passengers had to exit Malaysia and enter Singapore by foot, as the bus moved forwards slightly and wait for us to board again. We traveled south for another hour to a bus stop in what seemed like a deserted part of town. It was still dark and I couldn't see anywhere that was open. I got off the bus, collected my bag, and suddenly realised my first mistake: I hadn't brought any Singapore currency with me. I completely forgot that I would need to change my Malaysian dollars to Singapore dollars before setting off. As I contemplated my rookie mistake, I then realised this would make things difficult to get back to Malaysia. How would I pay for the bus ticket for the return journey? I didn't even know where to find the bus, let alone purchase a ticket. I had no bank card either. By this time all the other passengers got off the bus and wandered off into the darkness. I hadn't even noticed if they had hailed a taxi or another bus, I was too busy panicking about what to do next. I looked around in the darkness and saw nothing was open. I must be on the outskirts of town, I thought. This small bus stop was a strange place for a bus to arrive from Malaysia. My watch told me it was 4AM, which meant another couple of hours until sunrise. Maybe there would be people about then, and I could work out a plan from there. Eyeing a wooden bench to the side of the bus shelter, I decided the best thing to do was to wait it out here, and sleep until the rest of the world woke up.

I got a good couple of hours of shut eye. The sun was now starting to light up my surroundings. Waking up, I could see some distant office blocks with a few people walking around the outside, on their way in. Some shutters had gone up at the bottom floor units, revealing lights of general stores behind them. None of this was the Singapore that I had imagined, but then I knew I was some distance from the centre. I wondered if I had got off at the wrong stop. At least from here, I hoped, there would be a bus to get me straight back to KL.

From a distance, I could see a well dressed gentleman walking toward my direction. He wore a pink shirt and tie, thin rimmed spectacles and carried a leather business case. I stood up, brushed myself down and walked up to him. He was the first to talk.

"Good morning, where are you going today?" he asked in very good English, with a strong Singaporean accent. He could see that I was travelling, and probably guessed I was about to ask him for help. I told him I needed to get to KL, and asked if I could catch the bus from here.

"Oh,yes, this is the right stop. The bus will be coming soon."

"Ah, great, thanks! I wasn't sure." I then remembered my other problem. "Do you know if the bus takes Malaysian currency?"

"No, just Singapore Dollars. Do you need to swap currency? I can exchange some for you."

This was another example of how friendly and helpful I found people to be in this part of the world. He gave me a fair rate of exchange and we swapped just the right amount I needed to get the ticket. Sure enough, moments later a bus came along with "KL Sentral Bus Station" on the front. I got on, paid for my ticket and slumped down on a very relaxing seat - a nice contrast to the bench that my aching body could still feel. Just before I caught up on some more sleep, I pondered just how sometimes things seem to fall in place if you let it. This was especially noticeable when you were on the road.

As the bus arrived back in KL, I was reminded that perhaps there were quite a few more things that needed to fall into place for me, if I was to achieve my aim of returning to Sabrinah's village somehow. I really needed the universe to be on my side - going somewhere like Singapore without a clue or without any local currency, a very sympathetic universe was my only hope.

Getting to Subang airport was easy enough, and well in time for my plane. After checking in, I sat down with a coffee in the nearest seat that I could find. The airport seemed very busy, even in this smaller terminal, which was for the domestic flights to other places in Malaysia. I looked around and felt quite lonely for a change. Such a difference from being with the expedition crowd. Over the tannoy, flights and gate locations were regularly announced, in Malay before English. To my surprise I could start to understand everything before the English version came on. I confidently slung my cabin bag over my shoulder, and headed to the correct gate, destination: Kota Kinabalu.

It was a short flight of about 3 hours, and a good chance to drift away to the sound of The Police and Sting, and my newly found favourite Malaysian artist Zainal Abidin. Once the plane landed, and I finally got to touch the turf, being in Kota Kinabalu again felt great. It had that connection with me yet again, like no other place. This Borneo island was really quite something. It welcomed me back. I walked out of the airport, and hopped in a taxi to town straight away. Buzzing, not in the least bit tired. I was back!

Trucks & Buns

All I knew was to head for the *Stesen Lama*, or old bus station, to find transport back to Sabrinah's village. Lorraine had given me basic directions just before the end of the expedition.

"Head to the Old Bus Station and look for buses to Kudat. If you remember, that will take around 5 hours. Once you arrive in Kudat, you'll have to ask around for any transport to 'Bangau' - that's where the last shop is on the main road, before turning into the jungle. If you mention the village with the bridge, hopefully someone will be able to take you."

Her instructions were a reminder of how easy we had it before. We were always being transported around by Raleigh during the Expedition. None of us had to bother thinking about these basic things. Only now this was no basic thing. The level of English amongst the locals once in KK was much lower, and lower to non-existent once you headed out of KK itself. I knew I had to head north, though. Being the world's third largest island, that was going to be interesting. I had no maps with me.

The taxi pulled into a large car park area, separated from one of the main roads by a raised walkway lined with a few trees. The car park was littered with faded white minibuses, and one or two larger buses. A few hawkers were selling their wares by the walkway, mostly water and red bean buns. I felt peckish, so bought one. These buns were quickly becoming one of my favourite snacks on the go. As I chomped away, I could see people were dotted around, some squatting in the shade by the trees, others either standing by the buses or sitting in them. The buses had all windows and slide doors open. I could spot one or two guys walking from bus to bus with small wads of 1 dollar notes in their hand, talking to the passengers. I gathered these were the guys who sold the tickets, and headed towards one of them. There were no signs or indications of where each bus would be headed, or when. A classic bus stop in South East Asia, I thought.

"Most buses leave only when full," someone told me, as I remember. Heading anywhere here with a time-bound agenda would be impossible. Clearly, things like that did not work that way here. I would have to rely on my limited Malay to get around.

"Does this bus go to Kudat? I need to go to Kudat," I explained in my best Malay to one of the ticket guys as I approached him.

"Ooooh, Kudat? You want to go to Kudat? Ok Ok....you can speak Malay, very good, very good! Here...." He walked towards one of the other minibuses and beckoned me to follow. "I'll take your bag. Wow, it's a big bag. Let me put it here," he said, as he opened the boot door of the minibus. Somehow finding space to squash it in, he shut the door and gestured me to sit down in the bus. I thanked him, and climbed aboard. The seats were tiny, hard, and hot. At this time there were four other passengers sitting and waiting. Given that there were about 5 more seats to fill, I figured I'd be in for a long wait. I wanted to stroll around, maybe pop into a nearby cafe for a cold drink, but leaving the bus with my bag in the back was not something

I wanted to do at this stage. I knew that if I got out and simply collected my backpack, this would be seen by the ticket guy as a change of mind, and cause all kinds of puzzling questions. So, I resigned myself to the hard seat which was killing my back, and rested against the open window. I did what now became a habit, which was to write in my travel diary.

About an hour passed and only two more passengers got on, but thankfully the driver and the ticket guy deemed that sufficient to begin the journey. The ticket guy climbed into the bus and looked at me.

"Kudat where?" he said. I remembered that I should mention a place called Bangau.

"I need to get to a place near Banggau," I replied, unknowingly pronouncing the name wrong, with a strong 'g' sound. The guy looked puzzled. "Banggau?" I tried again. Someone behind me shouted unapologetically, "Ban*gau*...Ban*gau!*"

"Ah, OK....Bangau. Yes, Bangau!" the ticket guy replied. "Ok, I'll take you to Kudat first. You can maybe get another bus from there." I thanked him, and the driver promptly started the bus, which turned on the pitifully small internal fans above my head.

It was a precarious journey, compared to the last one I made. It seemed a life time ago, on that rickety bus with all my Raleigh team, heading out on our first project. How things had changed since then. And here I was, now on my own, doing my best to fulfill the promise I made to myself. So far so good - I renewed my travel visa, made my way to KK and was now on the right bus hurtling along a winding road which curled through the Crocker Range. The majestic Mount Kinabalu was to my right, towering above everything, looking like something out of a Tolkien book.

I could hardly believe I was on the top of that only a couple of weeks ago.

It was in the afternoon that our minibus made it to Kudat town itself. A smaller car park this time, surrounded by a long shaded bus shelter on one side, with a row of small stores on the opposite side. A few trucks were parked up - small cabs with large tarps covering the metal framed cage. Getting my bag, I walked towards the bus shelter - which was actually just a long concrete bench in the shade - to work out my next move. It was surprisingly easier than I thought, possibly because I was the only foreigner in the entire town, and so attracted all the attention. Mostly this meant lots of stares and smiles, but one guy seemed brave enough to walk up to me.

"Hello friend, where you from?" he asked. I replied to him in Malay. He switched to Malay straight away and started chatting. " Oh! You can speak Malay? That's good. Where are you going? What are you doing here?"

I explained that I needed to get to a village named Longan Besar. He hadn't heard of it. At least, not the way I was pronouncing it. I tried *Bangau*, and then told him there was a village near there with a bridge you had to cross by foot in order to get there.

"Ah! Yes, yes, I know this one with the bridge. Wait here!" He walked off to a few of the trucks, going from one to another. I guessed he was trying to arrange me a lift to where I needed to go. He came back with a pleased look on his face.

"Go here," he said, pointing at the third truck, "this truck will take you to the village with the bridge." Again, I thanked him and headed to the back of the truck. Inside the tarped back I could see two wooden plank benches which served as the passenger seats. I put my bag in and sat down. At least it was shaded from the sun, I thought. The driver came to the back and collected two dollars for the ride, and got back in the cab. The whole truck wobbled to life and started to move. It was my first time in one of these things. I had seen many of these 'people carriers' once we got near to Kudat district in my earlier journey. Obviously these were the normal way people got about from village to village. They were a whole new level of discomfort, but I was happy that I was finally being taken to my destination.

I shared this final part of the journey with three other passengers, who had various plastic bags of shopping by their feet. One of the bags jumped to life - it obviously had something living in there. I knew better than to ask, and besides, the truck journey was so noisy there was definitely no chance of any verbal communication. At different parts of what seemed like a long journey, the other passengers hopped off by the side of the road. I couldn't see too much since my view was only through the back of the tarp. The truck had negotiated a few muddy tracks to get to some of the destinations though, so I knew we had left the main road some time ago.

After a while longer, the truck went along another bumpy track before turning sharply to the right. Out of the back of the truck, I could see the sea on my right. I was sure we were about to reach the bridge I came here to build those months ago. Finally, the truck came to an abrupt halt, and the driver got out of the cab. He came round to the back to see me.

"Longan, Longan. We have arrived."

I stepped down from the back, grabbed my bag once more, and thanked the driver.

"Bah!" he replied with one of Sabah's most commonly used expressions. The truck promptly drove off back the way we had come, leaving a trail of dust in the air. I could see that this was the end of the road. That familiar bus shelter, and the beginning of the bridge. My bridge.

Axes & T-shirts

Putting my backpack back on, I made my way across the first part of the bridge. It felt amazing to be back, finally. I made it. It was strange to be here by myself though, with no friends from the expedition, and no project to focus on. What was I doing here? How would the villagers react to me just turning up? How would Sabrinah react? Each step on the wooden slats brought me closer to those answers.

As I approached the stretch of the bridge which spanned the estuary, I could see a couple of figures walking from the other side of the river. As they caught sight of me, they ran in my direction. The bridge wobbled from left to right as I heard their joyful screams, and my own name being called out. I recognised them as two of the younger children that always hung around our team as we worked. They certainly recognised me. "*Sam! Sam balik sudah!*" Not having a care for safety, they were jumping up and down, grabbing my arm and pulling me toward the opposite end of the bridge. Once they were happy that I was indeed walking in the right direction, they ran on ahead and darted off the bridge, round the corner and through some more mangroves shouting to all of my arrival.

I eventually caught up and crossed over the last bit of the catwalk that stopped at the beginning of the village. There was a mix of people just doing their thing - either swinging in the hammocks below the houses, exactly the same scene that I had experienced that first time. Only this time, people knew me. Lots of greetings and calling out from beneath the houses, welcoming me back. I walked in the direction of the Chief's house, thinking that would be the logical and most appropriate place to head to first. I felt a little bit uneasy - I was simply returning here without a plan, without any arrangement of where I would stay. Something told me I would be fine though, and it kept me going despite the awkwardness.

I could see that the picnic table and bench set that Ant once constructed for us outside the blue community hut, had now been moved to the patch of land in front of the Chief's house. A few people were sat around it chilling, chatting to more people swinging on hammocks under the house itself. Masnie was sat with Chief Apaun on the high veranda above, chewing on tobacco. As I neared, the people sat at the bench turned to see me. It was then that I could see Sabrinah, sitting there with her cousins. She looked at me and gave me a glowing smile. Will, Mainah and Anjas were also there, all looking my way with surprised faces.

"Sam! Group Satu! Welcome back, welcome back!" Anjas sprung off of the bench and ran towards me. "Sam. *Aso masalah* you come back. I'm happy for you. Come, sit."

He beckoned me to sit down, taking my bags off me and carrying them up to the Chief's house. He came running back down and sat next to me.

"Sam, you stay here? You stay at my house my father." Will exclaimed, only to be slapped by his sister Mainah.

"My *father's house!* Mulau ko!" she reprimanded him in his grammar. Everyone giggled, including me, and we continued a conversation that consisted of many questions aimed at me - what had I been doing since I left, where was Ant, where was crazy matata Ralph. Then they started asking me about *grup dua* and *grup tiga* - group two and group three - and what happened to the people in those groups. It took me aback just how animated they got about the three groups that had visited them and the apparent impact each group had. As they went over names, they would point at a section of the table, where each member had etched or signed their name. I suddenly remembered doing it myself, as all my group did. This table had become a time capsule, evidence of all the venturers that had come to stay and work here. Names and little messages in graffiti all over it. Will, Anjas, Mainah and Sabrinah were talking to me about each person, each name on the table, as if it were a museum piece of special memories. I felt a pang of jealously when it came to the names from group 2 and 3. I knew that they had been here of course - we exchanged catch up stories each changeover, and I was keen to get any news of the village - but now that I saw Sabrinah and her cousins talk about them in such a fond way, I realised it wasn't just about our first group anymore. Everything that had happened when we worked and played and lived here in those short three weeks, had been repeated for everyone in the village twice over, with different people. Some of the stories Sabrinah was telling me I had heard earlier at various points on the expedition, whenever different groups met up. It reminded me of one such story after meeting group 2 on a plane going back to Kuantan:

I looked back down the aisle of the plane to see who was around. My eyes fell on Dr. Ian - he had been working on the bridge with the second group, to carry on where we left off. What stood out as I looked at him sitting in his seat, was his shirt. He wore the blue and white *Sabah Boleh Malaysia Boleh* t-shirt that I had. I went over to speak to him and catch up. It was then that he told me about a young boy there called Jevelin - Sabrinah's brother.

"It was crazy! Some people came rushing up to me whilst I was working on the bridge one day. I didn't get what they were saying but they were pulling me back toward the village, so I followed them. It was this kid called Jevelin. There was blood everywhere, and I could see that he had cut his foot quite badly. He had been chopping some wood with an axe - even at his age! It's not my job to treat these people and be their Doctor, but I had to do something. He needed stitches. I cleaned the wound and sewed him up. He was pretty brave - no pain killers or any other medication. And that's why I got this T-shirt - Sabrinah came to me afterwards, so happy that I had treated her brother, that she gave me her shirt."

"Oooooooh jeaaaaaaalous!" Nigel shouted, overhearing our conversation. I admit it was funny and joined in the laughs, but yes, I was certainly jealous at the time. It was great that Dr Ian helped at that point - there were insurance and legal issues to consider. But this was in a village far from any medical care, and Ian didn't think twice. As a thank you, Sabrinah had given him the only thing she could - her newest t-shirt. He looked very smug wearing it.

Outside the Chief's house, we sat at that picnic table for some time. Story after story was being told. The sun started to set, which brought that amazing light across the village. With it, a different array of sounds coming from the mangroves and surrounding jungle, like subtle ringtones that play out different tracks every hour.

"Come, Sam. Let's makan, you hungry?" Will said as he stood up, signaling me to follow. I waved goodbye to Sabrinah and Mainah. Anjas had already wandered off to return to his house. I walked up the stairs of Will's house, happy in the knowledge that I had finally returned, and would have more time with Sabrinah. To talk, to know her more. I didn't know what I was doing, but it felt right. I walked into the main living room which I had spent so many nights before hanging out with Ralph. Chief Apaun was sat there. He stood up and spoke to me, mouth half filled with tobacco as usual, making it harder to understand.

"My father welcome you. You stay here in his house. You are his family. You are my family," Will explained. I was yet again so warmed by the hospitality instantly offered. Clearly, I was very special to Chief Apaun and his family. Will showed me to a bedroom. Unusually, it was a well kept room with small drawers, a desk and an actual raised bed on legs. An old wardrobe was in one corner, the doors damaged at the top and bottom. I guess nothing lasts long in this heat.

"This is my room. But now it is yours. Welcome, brother!"

I started to protest that I didn't want to take Will's room, but he wouldn't have any of it. Besides, he said, he had plenty of other places to sleep. By the bed, I could see that Anjas had placed my belongings already. It looked like I had no choice but to take this premium offer. Of course I had no choice - it was customary to treat guests extremely well. And, although I didn't know it yet, it was even more of an honour for the Chief's family to have a foreigner staying in their house.

Despite all of this, this action of me accepting the offer to stay with Chief Apaun had far reaching consequences that set off a chain of events, and led me down a path that would define the root cause of my struggles. Struggles that I had never faced before, and have never since forgotten. Looking back, though, I don't think it could have gone any other way.

For now, oblivious to any of this, I was happy to be taken in.

The Boat Trip

For the first few days, I got into the swing of being a part of Chief Apaun's family. It became quickly apparent that I wasn't allowed to help out or work in anyway. It was unfortunate, because this was the exact thing I wanted to do and experience. Besides, it was a way of paying my way for staying here. However, I came to understand that if anyone saw me 'work' then it would bring shame to the Chief's family, so I resigned to the fact that I couldn't do everything I wanted to do.

Another thing which was a taboo, was for me to wander off by myself too far. I often like to go for walks and stroll around by myself. This was fine within the village, and across the bridge to the beach. But any further, I would need a companion - especially if I was to go to another village, to the paddy fields or into the jungle. Chief Apaun was all too worried that something might happen to me. On top of that, it was unusual that I would want to wander around by myself. People here didn't really do that.

Often, Will was my companion, and would be happy to walk around with me. He liked it too, it was a chance for him to practice his English. Likewise, I would learn a lot of Rungus from him too. Hanging out in this way with a female would be out of the question - so any chance of going for a stroll along the beach with Sabrinah would never happen. The only chances I managed to spend time with her was within a group - maybe chilling under a house in the shade, or sitting around Ant's picnic table. Most of this would be limited to whatever words or phrases I knew in Malay or Rungus. She would always teach me and help me understand, but was reluctant to speak any English at all. Beyond words though, there was a deep connection that struck me each time. These interactions were all I could get, but they were enough to tell me what I needed to know. The effect she had on me when we first met on the bridge that day, only intensified each time. I did my best not to come across like some love struck teenager, but there was no hiding from it. Everyone around me knew, and would sometimes tease me, even in front of Sabrinah.

Sometimes Sabrinah would draw pictures, either in my journal which I often carried, or just in the dusty ground with a stick. It was an easy way to learn new words. She drew typical things you could see in the village. A house, a well, a clothes line for washing, nearby paddy fields, a water buffalo and so on. Everything was going so well. Until one morning.

I had woken up at the usual early time - not long after sunrise. Once the sun peeked over the horizon, the cockerels let you know about it. Breakfast was served, which I was always grateful for. Often it would be fried noodles or milo with crackers.

I wandered out and headed for one of the wells, near Mosuta's house, to freshen up. It was always my favourite well for some reason, and I had used it often to shower at and attempt to wash my clothes there during phase one. Through a gap between some houses, I could spot Sabrinah's house. I had never been there - it would have been very inappropriate for me to visit or just turn up. Mosuta came down from his house and sat on a log nearby.

"Sam, mandi?" *Sam, are you showering?*

It was quite common to ask questions that were obvious. Small talk. Yes, I was washing my face and hands. He noticed that I was looking towards Sabrinah's house.

"Sabrinah gone now. You will miss her?" he asked. I was shocked.

"Kenapa? Dimana?" *Why? Where?* These question words were often words I would use, even though I wouldn't understand the answer.

"I don't know," he shrugged. "Maybe KK, working."

I knew that it was common for people to head to KK for work - sometimes for months on end. Sabrinah had told me she did this before. I was shocked to learn of this now, and without goodbyes? I knew that sometimes things like this happened without the usual formalities of saying goodbye, but I sensed something was wrong. It just didn't feel right.

Back at the Chief's house, I asked Will where Sabrinah was, and he confirmed what Mosuta had told me. He was speaking in a very matter-of-fact manner, and changed the subject. He seemed guarded and showed as little emotion as possible.

"Oh OK," I replied, "Maybe she needs to work."

"Yes, she helps her father and younger brother," Will agreed.

I asked for how long, but he didn't seem to know. I thought it best to let this play out, see what was going to happen.

Later that day, Will's cousin Jukina came by. She would often be around Mainah, living in a house near the Chief's.

This suddenly became more of a permanent fixture, and she moved her things into Mainah's room, and now became part of the household. I thought nothing of it - she seemed pleasant enough, and it was someone else to talk to. Will's older sisters also made much more of an appearance than before - these were two ladies with families of their own, living nearby - I didn't know they were Will's family until now.

Over the next few days, things rapidly took a different turn. Will, and the Chief's family, continually made me feel at home and welcome, but now I suspected a strange agenda. I was sat outside late afternoon, when, as usual many others would relax and chat, enjoying the easier temperature the day offered at this time. Often, people would be talking in usual rapid Rungus which I little understanding of, but they would switch to Malay when speaking to me. And just like that, it started:

"Sabrinah no good!" Seoria looked at me. "She smokes. And she has many boyfriends in KK. She is not a good girl."

Seoria was Will's older sister, who had adopted Jukina. She was always a friendly figure, but this comment really threw me. I wasn't sure how to respond. Should I act surprised? Shocked? I certainly was.

"Yes!" she continued in Malay. "She has gone to KK now, back to her boyfriend. Many boyfriends. She is a playgirl, very naughty!"

Not the same Sabrinah I had come to know, I thought. I knew Seoria was not telling the truth here, but what I couldn't yet fathom was why. Opunga, the other older sister also joined in the conversation, agreeing and backing up everything Seoria had just said. It was odd that they both come out with these comments. Clearly, they both wanted me to forget about Sabrinah, and think ill of her.

Over the next few days, I carried on as usual, working through my thoughts on what to do. I had no plan, other than to let things play out, for now.

Asamping, Seoria's husband, took me out on his boat to a nearby beach a few bays away. Jukina followed. This was odd, and Jukina was behaving odd. She would talk to me but seemed awkward, uncomfortable somehow. And why would Asamping take just the two of us to the beach? I let it go, and tried to enjoy the trip. We sailed for about half an hour before we reached the beach he wanted to show me. He built a fire, and cooked some fish. The three of us had a pleasant time just chilling and chatting, then headed back onto the boat back toward the village. I knew Jukina was a friend of Sabrinah's, but when I asked about her, Jukina would just shrug her shoulders and say she didn't know, and then change the subject. I dropped it, knowing I wouldn't get anywhere. We returned back to the village, and back to Chief Apaun's house. I suspected nothing out of the ordinary, and other than this random boat trip, nothing out of the ordinary happened. Until the next day.

Poisoned Milo

The next morning, Noria came up to me whilst I was walking past her house. Noria was a relatively young lady, married to Rico, Will's older brother. They had two little boys. Noria was always very friendly to me, as was Rico, their constant joking around and laughter became a feature of our many conversations. As Noria stepped out of her house, this time she had a more serious look to her. Seeing that no one else was around at the time, she approached closer. She spoke in a quiet tone, as if to make sure no one could overhear.

"Sam. Please be careful!" She spoke in mixed English and Malay. Her English was surprisingly good. Apparently she learned from her father. "You know, Sabrinah is my friend. I care about her. Do not believe she is bad girl." I nodded in reply. Of course not.

"No, I don't believe those stories. But I'm not sure why they are telling them." I managed in my broken Malay. It seemed to work, she continued.

"This family, they are my family too, but they are no good, Sam. I'm sorry, but they speak bad about Sabrinah. They don't want you two together. They want you to marry Jukina!"

I laughed. But it was a nervous laugh. The boat trip yesterday made more sense now.

"But Sam, please be careful, ah? I must tell you something. I am ashamed of my family for being like this, this isn't fair for you. They give you magic, Sam." This was where the language wasn't clear. "Magic?" I queried. "What do you mean?" I knew what was coming.

"*Ilmu hitam!*" she replied. I knew that *hitam* meant black. I guessed the rest. Black magic?! What on earth was going on here. My mind was racing, trying to grasp sense of any of this. In any normal context, this would be something to laugh about. But here, in this village, normal was out of the window. I said nothing, hoping Noria would explain more.

"They make you have feelings for Jukina. It's very strong, Sam. So I tell you, do not eat any food from those sisters. Seoria or Opunga. If they offer you any food, it will be poisoned with *Ilmo hitam*. Do not eat or drink it!"

Ok, so now we are talking love potions. This was getting ridiculous. Absurd. But Noria was very sincere, and seemed genuinely fearful. To this point, neither of the sisters had given me any food or drink, so I figured whatever they wanted to put in my food hadn't been done yet. I thanked Noria for what she told me. I knew it took a lot for her to go against her own family like this.

"I tell you Sam, this is no good. But Sabrinah is my friend. She is a good girl. Remember, do not eat or drink anything!" I said I would not, knowing she was genuinely concerned. She returned to her house, and I continued on. Yep, this was nonsense. But at least it was nice to have confirmation from someone else regarding the false stories about Sabrinah.

By the afternoon, I was sat with the Chief and his wife outside on the veranda. We didn't say much - neither of them were that talkative – but we didn't really need to. I felt comfortable around them and did not feel the need to break long periods of silence with them. Just then, Opunga came by. She was carrying a plate of biscuits and a glass of milo. She passed it to me, and told me to eat and drink it. Prior to this, she had never offered me any food before. Was this a coincidence? Alarm bells in my head started ringing. I thanked her. Saying I wasn't hungry or thirsty when someone offers you food is simply not done. I felt cornered, and not sure how to react. OK, I thought. What Noria told me was nonsense. But still, I really don't want to eat or drink any of this! I hesitated. Opunga looked at me and smiled.

"Drink lah! It's hot today, you need some milo."

There was no excuse I could think of, other than to drink. How bad could it be? I didn't believe in any of this nonsense anyway, I knew what I wanted and no amount of *ilmo hitam* would have any affect on me. So I began to drink. Just enough to show I didn't suspect anything. Then I had an idea of how to get out of not having any more of it. Carrying the plate, I stood up, and explained that I would take it to my room to finish. I was tired and needed to lie down. I thanked her for the food and promised I would finish it later. It seemed to work. She knew I would be handing back the plate and glass, which would confirm with her that I had consumed it all. I hoped the thought of simply throwing the food and drink away when no one was looking was not a possibility that entered her mind. But that is what I did later on at night. As the evening came, I felt no different. I was sure I only had a little bit, and nothing would affect me. And as the night drew in, I thought I was in for another peaceful, normal night.

I'm not sure what time it was when I awoke. but it was far

from the morning. My room was shadowless, pitch black; outside brought no moonlight. It was the noise that woke me. Something to my right a few meters away, possibly outside the room . The sound was unfamiliar, a menacing growl that was ravenous and chilling, accompanied by gurgles and eerie cackles. The closest I could put to it was maybe a rabid dog, but as much as I wanted it to be a rabid dog, my mind would not allow that image to settle. Something much much darker, evil-like, was out there. And it wanted to come in.

I froze - actually I hadn't moved from the moment I awoke - and I was certainly unable to move now. Sleep paralysis? No, I had that enough growing up, and knew it well. This was different. At least I could move my eyes - that meant closing them in the darkness, which might help the noise go away.

It didn't.

Closing my eyes made no difference, since it was pitch black everywhere anyway. I tried to look around, find any familiar shapes that said I was still in the bedroom. Then fear gripped me even more, as it felt like I wasn't in my room. I wasn't anywhere. There was just a black, black void. The growling intensified. As if that wasn't enough, I could now see something floating towards me. It looked like a mangled up distorted figurine, like a really bad art project in pottery class.

This thing moved closer towards me. The growling continued, not coming from the figurine - it still sounded some metres away. The figurine floated closer. My mouth opened involuntarily, wide. I couldn't stop it. my jaw was aching, feeling like it could rip open at any minute. The figurine had a face. It was grotesque. It looked at me, came closer, and started moving towards my gaping mouth.

I tried to scream, but nothing in my throat worked. Not even a gargle. The figurine with the face floated to the opening of my mouth. My jaw stretched beyond its normal limits, causing a searing pain that threatened to rip me apart. In that vulnerable state, I became acutely aware of the absolute powerlessness that consumed me—a mere puppet at the mercy of this sinister entity. The growling escalated, morphing into a haunting wail that pierced the air.

And then suddenly, the figurine plunged into my body.

I convulsed. I wanted to throw up, but knew that wasn't going to happen. My jaw relaxed slightly, and then snapped shut, causing a searing pain through my teeth. The darkness around me suddenly started glowing hues of red and orange as my teeth grinded unbearably. Shapes were forming everywhere, floating upwards from the periphery of my vision. I tried to make out what they were, but I could not. Maybe skulls? I couldn't be sure. The growling spread all around me, like I was completely immersed in it. I felt my body starting to vibrate, my skin burn. A fever like I've never had before. It consumed me completely, and was the last feeling I remember, as the hues around me turned black again, as if everything was suddenly switched off, and the growling stopped.

Cutting The Net

When I awoke, I could feel my whole mattress was soaking wet. The memory of what happened that night was fresh in my mind. It was definitely one of the most intense nightmares I have ever had. Somehow, this seemed more real too. I can only say that it *really* felt like something had visited me last night.

Feeling my stomach, I turned onto my side, and heaved. Nothing. I heaved again, and brought forth the most weird black oily lumpy substance. Where did that come from?! I didn't want to think about it. Rather, I felt I had to wipe it up and throw it far away, which is exactly what I did. I dragged out the mattress, soaked in my night sweat, and left it to dry on the veranda. I placed the plate out for Opunga to collect, and took the tissue wrapped substance on a walk over the bridge, to drop it in the river below.

I do not know what happened that night. But what I do know is that nothing worked on me, whatever their belief system is. It angered me that someone should try to poison me with some kind of herbal concoction, with the intent on changing my mind about someone.

I stood there on the bridge, looking out across the water again.

I watched a solitary canoe boat slowly drifting out round the bend. It's owner gently working the oars to head out where the estuary widened. He had a mass of blue wire - fishing nets in his boat, ready to cast once he found his spot.

With the recent events, it felt like someone had thrown a net over me. But it was time to cut through it. What a situation to be in! It left me more determined than ever to see Sabrinah, and not let the Chief or his family to get in the way. I knew this would be difficult - especially from Noria's genuine fear - but I didn't care. It had been a few weeks now since Sabrinah had left the village. I couldn't just sit still anymore. It was time to cut the net.

It was the next morning when the seemingly crazy idea popped into my mind.

Go. Just go.

If there was ever a feeling to just follow this voice, it was now. I knew it was what I had to do. My plan:

1. Head to KK.
2. Find Sabrinah.
3. Ask to marry her.

Simple. I knew how I felt, and now I had to do something about it. The concept of marriage was an alien one for me. But meeting Sabrinah here had changed everything. One problem though: I had no idea where she was, and KK was a pretty big place. But something inside was driving me to do it, and I could not stop it.

Just go.

This was ridiculous, but logic meant nothing at this stage. I was on a mission and nothing would stop me. I packed my bag, leaving some things in the room since I knew I would come back at some point. I explained to Chief Apaun and Will that I had to go to KK and sort out some passport visa issues, that I would return soon. I knew this would not be suspicious in anyway - people would often head off to KK for all kinds of reasons, and if I went, at least I would not be under the care of the family whilst I was away.

I said my goodbyes and headed straight for the bus stop the other side of the bridge. As I climbed into the back of the truck that eventually came by, I thought again...I literally had no plan, no idea where to go, or where to stay. Was I mad? Maybe I needed to be.

A few people in the truck with me asked me where I was going - as people always asked in this country, much like the British talk about the weather.

"KK," I replied, which seemed enough of an explanation.

The truck eventually arrived and pulled in to the now familiar area of the Kudat bus parking area. It was easy to find a small minibus that was due to leave for KK soon. I boarded, and didn't look back. The journey felt its usually long self, winding through hills and bumpy roads. When the traffic started to get busier, I could tell we were not far from KK. Sure enough, after about 4 or 5 hours, we arrived at the very place I took the bus to find Sabrinah's village in the first place, Stesen Lama. As the bus finally parked up, I wondered which direction I would take. Perhaps just wander randomly around for a while. The situation dawned on me again, just how insane this was.

Nope. Everything will be fine. Stop living in doubt.

I picked up my bag, and as the driver slid the side door open, I was the first to step out. As soon as I put my foot down on the ground outside, I heard somebody nearby call out.

"Sam! What are you doing here?!"

KFC

I turned toward the voice calling my name. It was Linas, Anjas' older brother. I met him briefly, in the village, when he came to visit once. Thank goodness my Malay was good enough to communicate with him, I thought. I told him I had just come from the village, and was looking for Sabrinah.

"Oh! Sure, I know where she is. Last I heard she was working at the KFC branch in Centrepoint. Come, follow me, I will take you there!" he said.

I didn't think twice about what he was doing there on the very street where my bus had pulled up. KK was a big place, the capital of Sabah. And there he was at the right place, right time. Again, things were miraculously falling into place.

See? Just follow what you are feeling right now.

I followed Linas. That felt right. We walked through a busy part of KK. Everywhere seemed to be busy here, compared to Kudat. And especially compared to the village. This was a different world here, almost back to normality and civilization. And here we were heading to KFC of all places.

Entering Centrepoint, a big mall on a bustling corner not far from the sea front, I was glad to finally feel some proper air conditioning. It was not the most pleasant looking mall, but it certainly looked popular. People everywhere, shops left and right. I saw familiar brand names of the products they were selling - Nike, Adidas, Police sunglasses and Microsoft computers. As we went down to the basement level, I could see all the eateries. Familiar names of Pizza Hut and McDonalds were down here. We turned a corner - Linas knew exactly where we were going in this cramped mall - and there before us, was KFC.

"Ok, follow me, she will be inside," he beckoned as he walked straight in. My heart was beating fast now. What would I even say at this point? As we walked up to the counter, Linas started talking to one of the staff there. The staff walked off into the kitchens. I assumed this was to get Sabrinah to come out. But what I saw was someone else, a shorter, older Chinese woman. Linas spoke to her, and then she turned to me. Her English was quite good.

"Hello, I am the manager here. So, you are looking for Sabrinah, right? Yes she used to work here. But not anymore." Before all my hopes were dashed completely, she continued.

"She works for me directly, as my nanny. She looks after my children. Here -" she began to write an address on paper. "This is my address. You can go here."

I took the paper and thanked her. I am not sure what she thought of me, some random foreigner looking for a member of staff that she managed. But she seemed more than happy to give me her personal address, and told me what to ask the taxi driver. Very helpful. This would never happen in the UK. Another reminder of how different things worked out here.

"OK, I go now, OK?" Linas said, explaining that he needed to start his work soon. He gave me his address where he was staying. "After you find Sabrinah, come here and stay with us! My brother Anjas is also here at the moment."

I thanked him and we went our separate ways. Such a quick chance of a meeting that fell in place perfectly.

I headed outside into the heat again, to look for a taxi. Looking at the address the Chinese lady gave me, I smiled. Her address was at a place called "Beverly Hills Apartments". I didn't expect to see such a name all the way out here in Borneo.

Getting into a taxi, I gave the name to the driver. He seemed to know the place, and we set off. After about half an hour of heading out of the town centre, we entered a newly constructed area. On the right side of the road were older houses, on the left was a construction sight. A little further on past the site was a security gate and a posh looking sign "Beverly Hills Apartments". As we were waved in, I could see a few new shop units around. We turned a corner and came across the apartments themselves. Mostly red and pink coloured newly built apartment blocks, about four storeys high. They were in clusters, behind another security gate. The whole place was in a gated compound. Very posh looking. The driver indicated that he could not enter the compound, that I had to enter by foot. I paid him the metered price and he drove off. I didn't really know how to get back to town, but that wasn't a concern right now. I turned towards the security gate and showed the guards the apartment block number I had on my piece of paper. They pointed me in the right direction, and let me pass.

As I walked around, I could see the compound had a pool, a gym, and a basketball court for the residents to use. Not quite like the real Beverly Hills, I thought, but certainly a step up from what I had been used to the last few weeks. I found the apartment block I was looking for, and climbed the stairs to the upstairs apartment, number 203. There was the door. Had I finally found her? Deep breath, I knocked on the door.

The door opened, and there stood Sabrinah.

Beverly Hills

Time stood still for a brief moment. Then I snapped back into the present. There she was, standing in front of me. She looked pretty surprised herself.

"Sam! What are you doing here?"

"I've been looking for you. I wanted to speak to you," was all I could manage. Sheepishly, she opened the door wider and let me in. It was a nice tiled floor apartment, with much nicer furniture than I was used to. There were two kids sat in the main living area, the ones she was obviously being nanny to. She walked to the sofa and sat down. The kids went into their room to play with their toys. Something I hadn't seen for a while - the kids in the village had no such luxury.

I sat down next to her, trying not to shake. I wasn't good at small talk, especially in Malay. So I got straight to the point.

"I was looking for you, I wanted to ask you something," I said, trying to put a brave face on.

"Oh, what is it?" she asked.

I came out with it, in badly pronounced Malay.

"Will you marry me?"

She looked at me puzzled. In a comedic moment, I tried again, beyond belief that I fluffed this up. I think she got it the second time.

"Oh," she said with an embarrassed smile, and gave a rare example of a word she knew in English: "*wedding*," she said.

I could tell this was not an exchange to be expected, like I've seen a billion times in the movies. I had no idea how this was going to turn out, but glad I got there in the end. Sabrinah switched back to Malay, and gave me her answer.

"You need to go back to my village, and ask my father." This was her answer. Was it a yes? Or a no? Nothing was that simple. But of course, there was a right and a wrong way of doing things. One of those things here was to ask parent's permission first, as was very common in the UK many moons ago, and perhaps still is with some people. But here I was in Sabah, and there was no way Sabrinah could give me any kind of answer if I hadn't expressed my wishes with her father. I understood now.

"OK, I'll go back to your village, and ask your father."

She nodded, and smiled again. I felt I was almost there, that she would accept my proposal provided her father was OK with it. I hardly knew this girl, and she hardly knew me. I knew it was the right thing to do - the only thing to do. I said goodbye, and that I would see her soon. There was no farewell embrace, no contact of any kind - as was expected, just a well respected distance. She said goodbye and closed the door.

As I walked through Beverly Hills Apartments, I had this crazy notion that everything would fall into place, that we would be married, and living together in an apartment just like these ones. Almost *exactly* like these ones. I would have a job out here, and provide her with a lifestyle she would not have seen before. She would not need to be a nanny to someone else's kids. She would have her own apartment just like the ones here. Us two, in *Beverly Hills*.

Everything felt right. I'd done what I needed to do. What was next? Head back to the village, ask her father's permission, and all would be well in the world.

The security guards called a taxi for me, and I headed back to downtown KK. It was getting late, and there would be no buses leaving for Kudat until the next morning. I headed straight for Linas's place, to stay for the night. Sure enough, Anjas was there too, and we all went out for some dinner. Linas asked me if I found Sabrinah. I said I did, but I did not speak to them about what happened, or what we talked about. Although I liked Linas and Anjas, I thought it best to let no-one know of what was going on until I spoke with Sabrinah's father. I did all I needed to do for now, in KK. The next morning I said goodbye to the brothers and headed straight for the Stesen Lama, to get back to the village.

The journey back in the cramped minibus was uneventful, sweaty and long. Luckily the driver drove straight to the village this time, so there was no need to go to Kudat and get a different bus. I walked to Chief Apaun's house and placed my bag inside my room. The family were pleased that I had returned safely, and asked me how KK was. I told them that my visa was OK, and that I did everything I needed to do.

It felt nice to be back in the slow pace of the village, even if I had only been away for 2 days. I found an empty hammock and chilled with my journal, writing away all the things that happened. I didn't write much, my pen dropped through the netting of the hammock onto the dust and dirt below, and stayed there. My eyes had closed and was already way into whatever I was dreaming to even notice.

Coming round in a gentle breeze, I began to think. Sabrinah's dad, Kikiek, was a very friendly character, but also very shy at the same time. He was skinnier than most, and always seemed to be busy working at something, rather than lying in a hammock. He had a head of thick greying hair, and had eyes that were unmistakably Sabrinah's family. Speaking of family, it was only Sabrinah's father and younger brother Jevelin that I had seen. I had never seen a mother, or any other siblings. This was a little odd, since most families here had so many children, and a flurry of activity in each household. It never felt right to ask about her domestic situation. Sabrinah's house, which I had only seen from the outside, was very run down, parts of it patched up with scraps of wood. It was very quiet, and I didn't see many people going in, other than Jevelin running in and out occasionally. A big contrast to the other houses.

I hadn't spoken to Kikiek much at all during my time here so far. He was always smiling and laughing, but when he spoke it was very hard for me to understand - he hardly had any teeth left, if at all, which made his words muffled slightly. On top of this, he rarely spoke Malay. Many villagers of this age - I figured he was around 60 - didn't know a lot of Malay, and so only spoke in their mother tongue. The only time I heard anyone here in the village speak Malay, it was to me, since they knew that was what I had learned faster. They would also use Malay to speak to anyone else in the outside world, who was not Rungus. So the thought of having a serious conversation with Kikiek made me nervous - how was this going to work? Even going up to him, entering his house which was only two houses away from the Chief's, would easily arouse suspicion and get people talking. This had to be a meeting away from the eyes of the Chief's family.

I had an idea. Mosuta. He was one of my main allies, definitely someone I could trust. I knew he could help me with this. I walked over to his house and called his name from outside, hoping he was around. There were no doorbells, and I had never seen anyone knocking on doors the way we would - calling the name out from outside was the norm here. Thankfully, he was in. He popped his head out of the shutters of his house, and saw me.

"Ah! Sam! Sudah balik? Naik lah!" *Have you come back? Come inside!* I walked up the stairs and into his main living area. Mosuta's house was much smaller than the Chief's, and far more plain, but it was well kept. It was a newly built house - he had applied to the local council as one of the poorer members of the village, to get a council funded house. This sounded like a great idea. I was surprised to see that council houses were a thing, even here in the jungle of Borneo! What made it different to back home, was that the council would deliver the house to the successful applicant, in pieces. It came as a lego pack, and Mosuta had to build it. Most villagers here seemed to have the necessary skills to build their own house, so it was much cheaper to have it done in this way. Mosuta had told me earlier that Sabrinah's dad was soon to receive his, as they were one of the poorest families here.

I sat down on one of the cushioned chairs in the living room, and prepared in my mind how to tell Mosuta exactly what happened when I went to KK. He placed some milo and crackers on the small coffee table in front of me, and motioned me to eat and drink. Into my second cracker, I got straight to the point and began my debriefing. He waited patiently until I'd finished my story.

"I see," he began finally, "I help you, Sam. This is good. Sabrinah's father can come to my house, and we can talk here.

Better that no-one sees."

Mosuta was aware of how the Chief's family - particularly his two elder daughters Seoria and Opunga - were trying to manipulate the situation and get me to "marry in" to their family. Mosuta smiled and placed a hand on my back. "Don't worry. God will look after you." I was reminded how much a religious man Mosuta was. He did, after all, lead the Church service here every Sunday.

He said he would arrange Kikiek to come by later in the afternoon. I thanked him for his help, and agreed to see him later. The whole thing did seem a bit cloak and dagger, with secret meetings now going on, but I was in a very unfamiliar situation both personally and culturally. Rather than try to control it in the way I thought right, it was much better to allow things to play out with guidance from someone on my side. I returned to the Chief's house, and looked for something to occupy my mind until the afternoon.

The time finally got to 2PM, and I made my way back to Mosuta's house. It was the hottest part of the day, and even with the short walk to his house, I was still sweating profusely by the time I got to his steps. Calling his name again as I approached, Mosuta opened the door and welcomed me in. Kikiek was not yet there, so Mosuta and I just sat and waited. I wondered how it would go down, what words I would say. Mosuta noticed my agitation.

"Don't worry, Sam! Kikiek is a good man. There will be no problem." I did my best to relax. Moments later, I heard a call for Mosuta's name.

"Suta! Oooooh Suta!"

Mosuta replied. "*Mindakodno*!" Some Rungus I could understand - he was telling Kikiek to come up.

The door opened and in came Kikiek. I stood up and gave the usual greetings, and we all sat down again. Mosuta began talking to Kikiek, there was no chance for me to understand what it was. I could make out my name being mentioned, and Sabrinah's, so at least I could gather they weren't talking about the weather. This lasted for some time - longer than I would have expected - and as always, I was reminded by the situation to just be patient. As the exchanges were being made, smiles appeared along with momentary giggles, so I figured things were positive. Then Mosuta turned to me.

"Sam. I told Kikiek your intentions to ask his permission to marry Sabrinah." Just then, things felt even more real. I nodded. "Kikiek says it is up to her. Only Sabrinah can decide. It is no problem from him," he explained.

"*Aso masalah!*" Kikiek laughed in his usual way and put his hand on my knee. "If my daughter wishes it, then that is fine with me. I do not tell her what to do, or who to marry."

I was by now aware that arranged marriages happen, as much as 'normal' marriages do, here in Rungus culture. Parental permission, guidance and arrangements were still held in high regard and rarely to be challenged. It was a reminder just how much of a different world I was now in. I was very lucky that Kikiek's thoughts on the matter were very progressive. His permission was still needed - and given - but for him to simply say it was up to Sabrinah, was really quite a blessing. The meeting could not have gone better.

Kikiek got up, we shook hands and just like that, he left Mosuta's house and got back to whatever he was doing. I turned to Mosuta, who was grinning.

"See? No problem, Sam! Now, finish your Milo!"

Death

After getting over what felt like a huge obstacle, everything seemed better. Days passed into weeks in the village, largely uneventful. It was a time for me to write my journals, learn more Rungus and Malay, and wait. Forever, it seemed, for Sabrinah's return. She had to work to earn money, to support her younger brother Jevelin and her father. This was also quite a common thing to do here. There was no health care or homes to put elderly relatives in. Families would support each other and pool together every penny they earned, always focusing on making sure the most senior members were OK and eating well, or that the youngest still had a meal and went to school. Basic things like this were not taken for granted here.

The Chief's family suspected nothing of my proposal to Sabrinah, and I intended to keep it that way. This was the advice of Mosuta also. I just stayed in their house, and played along with being a polite and grateful guest. To be fair, they did treat me extremely well each day, and went out of their way to make sure I was OK. The sticking point was just their determination to split Sabrinah and I up, with the intention of marrying me into their own family via Jukina.

Will had gone to KK himself, so we had said our goodbyes.

He also had to work and add to his family's income. He was sorry to leave me, even though I told him not to worry about me. I reminded him that we were both the same age, in our early twenties, and I was fine to cope by myself. I did sense a struggle in his face as he spoke to me. Maybe he knew what his family - particularly his older sisters Seoria and Opunga - were trying to do to me, and my guess is that he was not in agreement with it. Due to his station in the family, there was nothing he could do, and was not able to speak out against it. I respected his position, and never spoke to him directly about it.

So these uneventful days continued as normal, until a day that was really not normal at all. It was a day which started like any other day - I strolled towards the village well for a morning wash, when Mosuta caught my eye. He was sitting on the edge of his house tying his shoes, looking like he was getting ready to go somewhere. When anyone puts shoes on instead of sandals, it means they are heading out of the village. He beckoned me over.

"Sam, today I go to my cousin's house. You come with me."

What would always sound like a command was actually a question, an invitation. Of course I accepted; any chance to go off on an adventure. I went back to my room to get changed, agreeing to meet Mosuta at the bridge. He had borrowed his cousin's car, and needed to return it, so it would be a ride in a nice cool air conditioned vehicle, to somewhere I hadn't been before.

Or so I thought. The rusted white Datsun Sunny was a shadow of its former self. As I went to open the passenger door, of course it wouldn't work. Why would it? Rather than give it a more forceful pull and risk the whole car disintegrating, I waited for Mosuta to get in and open the door from the other side. The seat wasn't too pleasant, but at least it was there. Experience told me things like seats, suspension or properly working steering are not all guaranteed. Mosuta put in the key, turned it and surprisingly the whole car shuddered to life. We headed off down the dirt track and reached the first bit of tarmac road, an hour away. Some time after that, Mosuta turned right, on to the main road which linked Kudat to the north, and Kota Kinabalu to the south. We were headed south to a village near Sikuati, where his cousin lived, about half an hour on this road. It was the main route to take for anyone going to and fro to the Kudat peninsular, and as such was well surfaced apart from some random parts, where without warning the road stopped being a road, and turned into rubble, had cracks the size of the Mariana Trench, or where one half had just 'slipped away'. For that reason, one had to remember to keep the speed down in fear of meeting any such obstacle. In Mosuta's cousin's car, going too fast was not an option. Besides, Mosuta always seemed to me to be a very cautious man. However, he would constantly squint as he drove, which concerned me since eyesight was a fairly crucial thing for driving.

It was then that I saw a large blue Toyota Cruiser coming toward us from behind, at speed. Mosuta didn't seem to notice, or at least wasn't phased by it. As the Cruiser got closer to us, it swayed to the right side, overtaking and brushing us aside like we were a wheelbarrow that shouldn't be on the road.

"Wah! Laju itu, Sam!" *Wow that was fast, Sam!*

Mosuta seemed halfway between impressed and shocked. I was neither. We continued on for a few minutes more, and approached a slight bend in the road. As we straightened up, we came across a sight that neither of us will ever forget. We slowed down in an instant, and we both jumped out of the car.

The Cruiser that had passed us earlier was now overturned, its once robust frame now resting in a crushed heap on its roof. Shattered glass littered the ground, and the side mirrors dangled precariously. There was no other car in sight; it must have spun out of control by itself. We approached the car and rushed for the doors. We got the driver's side door open easily, and we heard a voice straight away. A man was trapped inside, contorting his body in an attempt to reach us. We helped pull him out and away from the car. Mosuta gently laid him down at the side of the road. He was shaking, and didn't look good at all. There was no blood strangely, but the look on his face was one of someone who knew he was going to die. I have no medical training, but I could make an educated guess that this guy was not going to last. Leaving him with Mosuta, I ran to the passenger door to look for other passengers. The door wouldn't open, its frame shape was warped by the accident. Summoning all my strength, I tugged relentlessly, and Mosuta rushed to my side, leaving the first man lying there, breathing but fragile. Mosuta wielded a long wrench, which he skillfully maneuvered into the gap between the warped door and frame. I wasn't sure where he got it from. Maybe his cousin's car, though I didn't see him get it or know how much time had passed at this moment. We continued to pull at the door. Finally the wrench did its job, and the door prised open. We saw a crumpled body. Two more people rushed up to us, probably another car that had stopped on seeing the carnage. They immediately moved forward grabbed the body, pulling it out of the car while we pulled on the door. They dragged it away to the road side, near where the first guy was still lying there on his side. They lay the body of the second guy down carefully. One of them had retrieved a newspaper from his car, and placed a page to cover his face. That said it all.

Mosuta and I took a look into the car for anymore signs of life - we hadn't checked thoroughly in the mad moment of it all. Another lifeless body, soon brought out and covered alongside the second body. The other two helpers had called the emergency services. There was nothing more we could do. Mosuta told me that the other two were going to stay waiting for the ambulance to come, and that we should go. There was no concept of needing to hang around for witnesses to the event, they didn't seem to do things like that here.

Back in the car, we drove on in silence, trying to take in what had just happened. Neither of us felt the need to say anything for a while. We got to Mosuta's cousin's house; there was no-one there, so we just left the car and walked on back to the main road and waited for a bus. It was understandably a very solemn moment.

"Sam. It is strange when you see death. Its picture stays in your eye, your heart."

I didn't need that translated any more. I knew what he meant. As we rode in the back of the truck which had picked us up, I pondered how rare this would be back home. Emergency services are much quicker, and any bodies at the scene are soon taken away. The accident is usually swept away before anyone can see. 23 years in the UK, I don't ever remember seeing anything like it. It only took 6 months into Malaysia. But that was enough, I didn't need to see any more.

Unfortunately, the events of the day were not over by a long shot. We finally arrived back at the village and had just crossed the bridge, when a couple of children came running up to us.

By their faces, we could tell something wasn't right. They were talking too fast for me to understand any of it, so I waited for Mosuta's explanation. He had dropped his head, and ushered the children back into the village. He turned to look at me. It didn't look good at all.

"A little girl has died today," Mosuta spoke slowly and softly. "They have returned her body to the family house, from the hospital. It's Ongijal's daughter. Come."

He picked up pace and I followed, walking through the village to the family's house. We could see that many of the villagers were gathered around, all subdued and silent. I could hear soft wailing coming from inside the house. I knew it to be Ongijal's house. His daughter, aged only 10, had passed away in the local hospital from dengue fever. We went inside his house, where people were sat in various groups, silently. A coffin was open, in the middle of the room. Ongijal and his wife were kneeling beside. I was not sure what the protocol was in this situation, but I went up to Ongijal and put my hand on his shoulder. He looked up at me and clasped my hand, saying nothing. His daughter lay there in the coffin, her face much more puffy than I remembered. I didn't see much peace in the face. It was too traumatic to see a child like that. It seemed so wrong. I knew of this girl from the time we built the bridge in phase one. She would always play around us, watching us at work.

After some time of being in the house, we heard some calls from outside. Some of the older brothers of the family had finished digging a grave situated by the church. She was to be buried straight away. In normal circumstances, the deceased must stay in the house overnight before burial. However, if the cause of death was a disease or infection of any kind, then burial needs to be much quicker, according to traditional customs.

We all headed over, Ongijal's other children carrying the casket. Gathered around the grave site, Ongijal's wife placed some toys and a bag of clothes into the casket, before finally closing the lid. Placing the toys of a child into a coffin seemed to be the last thing parents let go of. They lowered the coffin carefully down, and began covering it with dirt. Everyone was silent save the mother, the only one making a noise, sat by the hole in the ground, being slowly filled by her older children. It was the first time I have heard and seen the grief of a mother losing a child.

Soon after, everyone proceeded back to Ongijal's house. Food was being prepared, and noise returned as people sat in groups talking quietly, playing cards or chess, or just sat chatting. No rice wine in sight – any alcohol in the village would be banned for a while, out of respect. But this flurry of activity was a strange sight, not one I would expect from a funeral. It lasted 3 days and 3 nights. Everyone just stayed around the family, chilling. Even some laughter amongst the chatter. It was like the whole notion of being too sombre was not required, not necessary. The grief was there of course, but not in the way I was used to seeing. Everyone here all kept Ongijal, his wife and his children company each day. That was part of their way of grieving. Being a community.

Secret Meetings

Finally, the day came when Sabrinah returned. I watched from Mosuta's house, sitting on his steps outside. I wanted to rush over, but of course couldn't. Heading in the direction of her own house, she stopped by others as people leaning out of their open shutters were waving at her and chatting away.

"Don't worry!" Mosuta patted me on the back. "Everything will be OK. Wait for Sabrinah to settle and meet her father. We will arrange a meeting in secret to discuss the engagement. Pawai will come!"

I guess I shouldn't have been too surprised that all this arranging had been going on behind the scenes. I was reminded to stay patient, and let things happen the way they should. Pushing too hard with my typical western impatience would definitely not work here. The mention of Pawai was very reassuring. He was someone I had met some weeks ago, in a nearby village the other side of the bridge. His English was very good, and when I first met him at his house weeks ago, when Mosuta took me over, he explained why.

"Hello Sam! I have heard so much about you!" I was so surprised to hear someone speak to me in English. It felt like it had been a long time since this had happened. It was.

"My name is Francis Pawai, you can call me Pawai. I am the local administrator here, working at the Kudat Town Board. I heard that someone from the Raleigh group had returned to the village. How interesting! I wondered why anyone would do that - someone is interested in our Rungus culture, hmm?" he started laughing, shaking my hand. He then invited me in to his house. It was a larger house than normal, overlooking the beach. I could tell this was a man who had achieved more than the average person, not least due to his level of English, but to have a house like this, and two cars outside also said something. We sat down on much more comfortable chairs than I had been used to.

"Or," he continued, "maybe you returned because of a certain girl?" He laughed again, as did I, although slightly more uncomfortably. "Don't worry lah - we Rungus know everything, we can read the minds of everyone. We are not just simple people, some of us know the old ways." He laughed again, tapping his nose. His wife and daughter busying themselves with preparing drinks already. I wasn't sure if he was joking about the mind reading, but he certainly had heard right about the reason I returned.

After establishing I was from England, he became animated and very keen to tell me that he had studied at the University of Norwich some years ago. This explained his level of English. He lived there with his wife for 3 years, and then returned having completed his degree to sit as a deputy administrator at the town council in Kudat. He was also partially responsible for the liaisons between the Kudat Town Board and Raleigh, in identifying the bridge repair as one of the projects for Raleigh to work on. So in part, it was down to this man Francis Pawai that I ever came to Sabrinah's village in the first place!

I met with Pawai regularly over the last few weeks, and although he was a busy man, he always made time for me. We developed a great friendship, and apart from Mosuta, he was the only person I confided in regarding my struggles with Sabrinah, and the Chief's family. He was a patient man who listened and gave me a lot of advice. Being able to speak English so well was a huge benefit, and helped provide an invaluable insight into not only my situation but also Rungus culture in general. After our many meetings, I made lots of notes in my journals to remember the things he had explained and stories he told me.

It was a great relief to hear that Pawai himself was going to be at the meeting. He would be a great mediator and translate anything I did not know or understand. I could also tell that many of the other villagers appeared to have a lot of respect for the guy. Mosuta explained to me about what would take place at the meeting.

"We will meet later in the evening, near the community hut. This is far enough away from the Chief's house, they must not know. We will discuss the arrangement of your engagement, and the *buruh*."

I didn't understand this last word, and Mosuta had to explain that it meant a payment for the wedding. I understood this to mean dowry - a payment, essentially to be paid for by the groom, to the bride's parents. This was a system common in many countries across the world, which included all the indigenous tribes here in Borneo. The dowry payment could be a sum of money, property, or even livestock. Thinking back to the UK, as I was growing up I, the normal thing to do was for the bride's parents to foot the bill of the wedding. Not too dissimilar to here, since the money part of the dowry was often used to pay for the wedding and all its trimmings.

The evening came by quickly, and I waited for sundown to head across towards the community hut, the Chief's family seemingly unaware of any of this. As I arrived nearby, I could see a table had been placed outside on an area of ground which a few houses encircled. It acted as a perfect place for any private meeting, shielded from any onlookers elsewhere. I was led to the table by Ongijal who had come to meet me, and saw that Kikiek was there with Sabrinah, along with Mosuta. Ongijal also joined, and sat down at one end. Sabrinah gave me a glance and beamed a smile at me, which did its usual trick of putting me in a trance. This was the girl I was about to agree to spend the rest of my life with. I had no doubt.

We waited for Pawai to come, who eventually did, with his wife Jalima. After the usual warm greetings, they sat down and some conversations began to take place. Things seemed to be going very well, despite the only people not talking were myself and Sabrinah. It was definitely a conversation for the grown-ups, it seemed. I could tell that Pawai was explaining to Kikiek the problems I had been facing with the Chief's family, and that my efforts to find Sabrinah and not be swayed was a testimony of my determination and courage. He was giving me a good reference, and I guess this was necessary - Kikiek did not know me that well, and after all, I was a foreigner. Nobody here had any experience of dealing with foreigners - not least the idea of having one become part of the family! This was all new ground to them as much as it was to me.

Just then, I heard some commotion coming from nearby. Some voices were raised and were coming our way. It was Seoria and Opunga. They had somehow found out about our meeting, and were far from happy. Walking up to the table, talking quickly and noisily, being unusually animated with their expression, their arms flailing about. I hadn't seen many people here this angry. Ongijal got up and started to talk to them, but they were clearly ignoring him. The whole atmosphere changed completely. It seemed they aimed all their efforts at Sabrinah, shouting at her non-stop. She understandably winced - it was an awful situation to be in, a constant barrage of wind and noise coming from these two awful ladies. I could tell they were talking about me. It was only later that I learned about the comments they were hurling at her.

"What are you doing here?! You think this guy Sam will look after you? You are mad. He will take you back to his country and sell you! You will never be seen again. And do you really think that he likes you? Why would he?! Ha! You are the poorest family here. You dont even have a pillow to rest your head. He would be embarrassed to be in your house!"

And so the accusations and comments went on, despite others trying to stop them. Although I became very angry inside, I knew better than to show it. I was more focused on Sabrinah and how terrible it must have been for her to be at the receiving end of all that. Seoria and Opunga finally stormed off, confident they had done the damage they set out to do, leaving us all at the table in relief. We continued the conversation for a short while more, though it felt noticeably different. It was brought it to a close on the understanding that Sabrinah would take some time to consider everything and, hopefully, accept my proposal. I thanked her and everyone present, and the meeting came to an end. Pawai apologised for the interruption, even though it was nothing to do with him.

"But do not worry, Sam. Those two ladies are really quite

determined to meddle and mess with you and Sabrinah. But we discussed everything despite that, and it was all clear. Sabrinah will give you her answer in a couple of days. I am sure she is fine with it."

I thanked him and said goodbye, not sure that anything would go the way I wanted it to now. I fought with a sinking feeling.

Quit worrying, it will turn out fine. No doubts, remember?

That reassuring feeling inside me doing its best, though my head was full of worry. I walked back to my room, feeling defeated.

The Lonely Pier

Tonight was a birthday party in one of the houses. I, like everyone else, joined in the festivities into the night. There was music and dancing as usual. I put on as cheerful a face as I could. But I could not focus on much at all. I was still waiting for Sabrinah's answer. Strangely, she wasn't at the party. I felt something was wrong, but knew that it would not have been appropriate to go and look for her.

Finally it was Mainah who came up to me, and spoke in my ear. Sabrinah was waiting outside near the river, she said. I got up immediately, and snuck out of the party towards the river. There she was, sitting on a small wooden pier perched over the water. The moon was out full, sneaking its light through parted clouds. The noise of the party continued as I got closer to the pier. At least there would be no eavesdroppers here. She sat there with her feet drawn in, clasping her knees and deep in thought. In this rare occasion that we had completely to ourselves, I sat down next to her and asked her how she was feeling. I guess I didn't need to ask, the troubled look on her face was enough to know.

"I'm sorry, Sam. I cannot be with you. I am no good for you, and we are too different, you and I. I'm sorry. I have to leave tomorrow, return to KK. So I will say goodbye now."

She turned away, obviously finding it hard to look at me, and stood up. I knew better than to ask why, what happened, what changed, please don't leave, it will be fine, don't listen to those others. None of that would make any difference. There was nothing I could do, and I knew it. The Chief's family had got to her.

She walked away towards her house, into the darkness, leaving me sitting alone on the pier.

Stars & Shamans

I took a walk away from the noise of the party, and reached another house further down the river. I slumped into the empty hammock underneath. Its rope was stretching and creaking as I swung my feet up, my arms hanging limply to the side, heavy. Everything was so heavy. My mind was racing, pounding, struggling to make sense of it all. After everything that happened, after everything I did, I felt destroyed, defeated now. Alone. Even the mosquitoes left me alone. They knew better than to bite me this night. A couple of hours passed, the party was over. The air was still, only my hammock swinging by my weight. No one would bother me in this late hour – most of the villagers would stay in their houses after dark, and it was past midnight by now.

I couldn't properly process what was going on now. I was wrong. But how could I be wrong about this? I was so convinced that everything was going ahead. But her answer was no. That was it. Time to move on.

Closing my eyes, the conversation we had on the pier echoed in my mind. Something wasn't right. Her tone of voice, the way she looked at me. But it was too late. The Chief and his family had got their way – I don't know how they managed it, but it worked. They won.

No they haven't. You're fine.

I ignored that. I wasn't ready to listen. I felt the need to head further away. Swinging out of the hammock I slipped my sandals back on and took a walk out of the village, towards the bridge. The moon was struggling to shine her light through the heavy low clouds that hung around, watching me as I dragged my heels across the wooden walkway. The nocturnal noises of the surrounding mangroves got louder as I neared the bridge. Not so much a constant chatter but more sporadic beeps and tweets, a dialogue between insects and creatures unknown to me. Perhaps they were discussing my presence, observing a solitary figure wandering at an unconventional hour? Maybe not. Maybe they knew I needed to keep going, they were all friendly noises and would let me pass.

The village now in the distance behind me, the bridge did its usual groaning and creaking as I started to cross, only louder this time since it was so late. I didn't know where I was going, where I wanted to go. Just to go. One foot in front of the other. The noise of the sea was now drawing me closer, so I headed that way.

The tide was in, but there was still plenty of beach to walk along. This familiar bay seemed so dramatic now, in the dark. The clouds had shifted to reveal the huge expanse of the night and all its stars. Strange like that, I noted, that the sky could change at a moments notice. I walked for a good couple of kilometres, until I saw a piece of washed up driftwood, and sat down on it. I dropped my head again, defeated. I could walk far away from this mess now. Accept what happened, get on a bus tomorrow and see where it would take me. Get on with things, leave this all behind.

No. Not yet. Look up.

I breathed in and let out a big sigh. Why would I do that? Giving in, I directed my gaze upward, my eyes now accustomed to the darkness. Extra stars revealed themselves one by one, until they formed vast clusters that seemed to span the entire expanse of the sky. I sat incredibly still, looking at the universe unfold before me in all its vastness. And just like that, it showed something to me. I felt the entire night sky fill up inside me. I saw an image of Sabrinah, her face adorned with a radiant smile, holding a child in her arms. I closed my eyes and emptied everything, all my thoughts and doubts. I almost let out a chuckle. Is this what the old ladies see in the tea leaves of your empty cup? I must be on the brink of madness.

See? I told you.

By the next morning, the effects of what I saw last night withered away to the back of my mind. I wasn't sure if that was a conscious process or not, but regardless, I had to get up and do something. My head was spinning. The best thing for me was to get out, and go for another walk. Although the incredibly slow pace and tempo of village life had long since taken its effect on me, there were times when I had an uncontrollable burst of energy and just wanted to move, run, to get things done, to go against the insane heat and humidity that everyone here endured every day of their lives. As I stepped out of my room into the communal area, there was the usual flurry of activity – Mainah and Jukina were at the stove cooking something, a few of the younger kids running through the house, Masnie was sat on the veranda, shouting occasionally at the kids. I walked past her and gave a courteous smile. Chief Apaun was nowhere to be seen. The tension was more obvious now – he and his family had played their major card, and it seemed to have its effect. Sabrinah had gone, for a second time. Sent away, probably to the city again to work, to be out of the picture. They had got to her, and it was too much for her to handle.

Descending the stairs to the house, I gave a nod to Masnie, and explained I was going for walk. I walked out off towards the rice fields. I tried so hard to follow the rules, to be patient. It got me nowhere. I stormed on, allowing my anger to quicken my pace despite the heat of the day. I reached an old hut, or *pondok*, which acted as a resting place for anyone working the fields. I climbed up and sat on the bamboo flooring, grateful for the shade. The paddy fields opened up before me, right up to the foots of the hills in the distance. It was beautifully green here. And a great chance to work on my next steps. KL? I had a few friends there - Saini, Minne, Gemma. Or maybe just move on, go somewhere new? Home wasn't an option, I wasn't ready to face Leeds anytime soon. But funds were running low. I couldn't yet make a decision. Still not sure of what to do, I turned back towards the village, happy to have sweat out a good walk at least.

On my return, I passed by Mosuta's house, threw a bucket of water over me from the well to cool off, and sat down for a while. He came out and sat nearby on his steps.

"Don't worry, Sam," Mosuta gave his usual encouragement. "Don't worry." He couldn't say much else this time.

"I'm not worried," I replied finally, "I just have to accept it and move on." My mindset had switched, I was in a mode fully prepared to leave. As soon as I worked on a plan.

Two days had passed, and I decided to pay a visit to my friend Pawai. He always told me to come by any time I felt like it. Today, I would take his offer up. Besides, it was always a welcome change to speak in English. We sat for a while over drinks.

"Come with me today," Pawai suggested, finishing off his *teh tarik*, a kind of milky chai tea. "I want to take you somewhere special."

I was still feeling pretty low, everything beyond my control. Drifting now without a sail, without direction. I needed distraction, so I nodded as I sipped my own drink. Before I could finish it, Pawai was already heading out to his car. He was one of the very few around here that owned one (or two, in his case). Being on the senior team of the local town board obviously had its perks.

Pawai started the engine, and the car with its amazing air conditioning came to life. It felt so luxurious to be sat somewhere feeling cool, when all around was sweltering in the heat. Car journeys were amazing here, for that reason alone.

"I want to take you to a longhouse – it's a very old one, but I want you to see the way we used to live not so long ago. Now many of us Rungus eventually moved out of these longhouses, and have our own dwellings and so on, but before, when we first moved into a clearing in the jungle to settle our village, we always lived together for protection. You will see!"

I had seen these longhouses and knew about them. Some villages still had them – the other Raleigh team had a project to build a modern longhouse for the inhabitants of the village they stayed with, a few miles away from here.

The drive took us back on the main road for a while, before heading off down another dirt track, winding its way through jungle and dense greenness everywhere. Finally, we pulled up at the edge of a couple of dwellings. Sure enough, as I got out of the car I could see behind these dwellings began an enormous long house built upon stilts, about six feet off the ground. All its roof was heavily thatched from materials taken from the surroundings. There was no corrugated iron to be seen, no evidence of modern materials. I could see some movement inside, though it was very dark to see clearly. Pawai called out, and received a prompt reply. At that point I noticed an old lady appear in the doorway. She was dressed similar to the elders of Longan Besar, the typical Rungus black body-sarong, but with a greater number of beads and bands all over. By her feet, I could see that to access the longhouse, there was a log leading upwards from the jungle floor to the doorway, with well worn grooves cut into it. This pretty much acted as the stairs to enter the dwelling. The log acted as a drawbridge, which could be withdrawn if any unwanted visitors were nearby.

The lady beckoned us up. Once inside, my eyes slowly adjusted to the darkness – I was surprised how dark it was. The floor comprised of bamboo slats, which stretched along a corridor to the other end of this long dwelling. The outside wall was a lattice which let some light in, and a little welcome breeze. On the other side of the corridor was another interior wall, but this time with several doors at regular intervals all the way down to the end. These were the individual family dwellings. The lady motioned us to sit down on the bamboo slats, near to the outer wall. As we sat, some of the people who were in the shadows went quickly back into their rooms, seemingly very shy of strangers.

She spoke very softly to Pawai, he nodded his head in acknowledgment. I relied on him to translate for me. Typically, the older the speaker, the older the words uttered. Younger generations of Rungus might still struggle to understand, I later learned. This lady was definitely old. She sat opposite us both. As the light from the side wall shone onto her I could see that her black sarong had bright colours stitched in various places. Her neck was completely covered in many beaded necklaces, that must have weighed a great deal. Even more heavy were the brass coils wrapped around her lower arms, covering her skin from her wrist to near her elbow. Her face was filled with lines of experience and wisdom - she looked every part the village shaman. I guessed right - Pawai explained to me what she was – a *Bobohizan*, in Rungus culture. A Rungus priestess, loosely translated. Her eyes were very distant, and she had a very calming presence as she moved and spoke. As for her actual age, I really had no idea.

She continued to speak to Pawai, he giving short nods in reply, once she paused. During this time she barely focused on me, as if I wasn't in the room, so I really had no idea what she was talking about. I just sat patiently and took in my surroundings. By now a couple of children popped their heads out of the rooms, and came into this huge communal corridor. Some adults shyly followed and sat down. They said nothing, but sat within earshot, curious of the foreigner that had come to visit.

Finally, Pawai turned and spoke to me.

"This lady says she knows about you, about your situation."

I didn't know what to do apart from look at her, smile, and nod. The best thing to do in Asia.

"She wants to show you one of our old traditional things that we have."

She placed into my hand what looked like a wooden stick with rope and beads.

"She said this is a very old puzzle, and with it comes a story. It goes something like this, if I can understand her correctly – even she is using some words that I am unsure of! There was once a poor boy who wanted to marry a girl of a much higher station. This would not normally be approved, but he persisted, and the parents gave him a puzzle to test if he was clever enough for their daughter. Well, something like that, anyway!" Pawai nodded towards the puzzle I held in my hands, inviting me to the challenge.

I looked down at it, inspecting it a little closer. There was a sense of recognition. I *knew* this puzzle. I picked it up and looked at it in the light. It was a stick about 12 inches long, with a rope in two hoops tied to it. On each hoop was a threaded bead. The idea was to somehow get both beads on one hoop. Normally this kind of puzzle would seem impossible - you could be fiddling with it for ages and never solve it. But there it was, in my hand, and it triggered a long lost memory from my past. My father often built and played with puzzles of his own, fascinated by how they work and how they can confuse people. He would give puzzles to guests who came to visit. Needless to say, I spent my formative years playing with these puzzles. This one in my hand was *exactly* the same as the one my dad put into my hands all those years ago.

Now, sat in a longhouse on the other side of the world, opposite an old lady I had never met before or understood, the exact same thing happened again. Only I was the guest in someone else's house. Without thinking, my hands working on more of a muscle memory than anything else, I manipulated the puzzle, twisted it and pulled it, and got both beads on one hoop within moments. I gave it back to her, completed. Pawai laughed out loud, not believing what he just saw. By contrast, the *Bobohizan* had no reaction in her face. She spoke again, this time looking at me, now showing some flicker of satisfaction. I waited for Pawai to translate. He stopped laughing, and cleared his throat.

"She said Sabrinah will return in three days."

My Left Foot

Back in the village, I said nothing and told no-one about what happened. I didn't even know what to make of it myself. I just quietly went about the usual tasks of helping with the household chores (the ones that they let me do, anyway), and sitting and chatting with different people from the village to get through the long day. I decided not to hope, not to listen to any nagging smug voice inside my head. My return flight to the UK was coming up soon, but I couldn't think about that now. If I could get a visa extension somehow, I would. I could explore the rest of South East Asia, if I had the money. Unfortunately like everything else, my finances were running out.

The third day came since my meeting in the longhouse. It started like any other day in the village, and despite all the strange things that had happened to me so far, I had spent the last two days deciding that enough was enough. Ignore anything that anyone said, and get ready to leave.

Towards the late afternoon, there was something going on near the bridge. I looked from a distance. Through a gap in between a house and some trees, I was shocked to see Sabrinah, walking towards the Chief's house. I watched from a distance. She stopped below the house, and looked up to speak to Chief

Apaun, who was sat in his usual perch on his veranda. I wondered what words were exchanged, but as usual, it was impossible to tell even if I could hear what was being said; the body language and facial expressions of Rungus people also contribute to being lost in translation! A few moments later she continued on to her father's house to drop off her bag, and then returned to Apaun's house and climbed the stairs to enter. I sat still feeling it was not yet the time to go over and say hello. I had no idea of what was going on, and refused to make any predictions. It would take a lot of patience to get through the day without pushing to find out, but I managed to hold out until Rico, the Chief's older son, came over.

"Hey Sam, *apa kahbar*?" Smiling as he approached me. "My father wants to speak with you. Can you come?"

"Boleh!" I said in the most cheery way possible, attempting to cover up my nerves. We walked over, and climbed the stairs to his house. As we walked in, I saw that the Chief and a few of his family members were sat around the perimeter of the room. Sabrinah was also there, sat next to Masnie. She gave me a quick glance with a usual timid look and smile that reminded me that all this was worth it. Seoria and Opunga were also there. I couldn't read the expression on their faces. I sat down. Rico sat with me, taking on the role of Will who had not yet returned, interpreting the parts of the Chief's speech I did not understand. By now I could pick more up, but still needed Rico's help the majority of the time.

The Chief spoke at length, uninterrupted. The occasional nod or 'mmm' in agreement from other members of the group were the only other responses they showed. Listening to him, even before Rico translated for me, I realised the tables had finally turned. The two sisters Seoria and Opunga apparently had gone to KK to find Sabrinah and apologise. Sabrinah and I had the blessing of the whole family. Chief Apaun agreed not to interfere anymore, and accepted that I had no desire in marrying anyone he considered 'valid' in his family. If Sabrinah and I wanted to marry, it was allowed. Sabrinah was, he pointed out ironically, actually part of his extended family too, and I was therefore a welcome addition. I decided not to speak - I wasn't expected or invited to – so my urge to make any reference to him having double standards was kept inside. That was the western part of my upbringing. Argue, complain, point fingers, accuse and justify. Even if you've won. None of that was necessary here, and would have been wholly inappropriate anyway. Once Rico confirmed my translations were correct, I looked at Chief Apaun and nodded my understanding.

Over the next few days, Sabrinah spent much more time in the Chiefs house, now that everything was in the clear. There was no more stress, fear or secret meetings that had to take place. A weight had been lifted. Still, there was much to do. My visa was going to expire soon – I had only a week left, and had already extended it once. My flight back to the UK was booked. I did not want to leave, but I knew that it was an important step towards the beginning of a new life. In this last week, we were to become engaged officially. Sabrinah's father had decided it should be the 5th of the month, because he liked the number 5. Preparations were being made rapidly, but again I was not expected or allowed to help out.

It was late at night on the 4th, when I turned in and prepared for bed. Unfortunately there was one more bit of drama to endure. All of a sudden, I felt a searing hot pain coming from my foot.

It was unbearable. I wrestled with the pain and rolled about, falling off my bed. I heard footsteps approach, and the door opened.

"Sam! Sam! *Kenapa*?!!" Half the Chief's family ran into my dimly lit room. They were asking me what was wrong after hearing all the commotion. I couldn't speak. I could only clasp my leg and try to cope with the increasing pain. It felt like a poison travel slowly up my leg, inside, reaching other parts of my body. Masnie's face hardened with determination as she quickly rubbed a silver necklace on my foot, where the core of the pain had started, whilst mumbling to herself words I did not recognise. My heart beat started to increase, I felt hot. Voices around me were panicking.

"Stay calm!" I thought to myself, "just stay calm!". Was I going into some kind of shock? I wouldn't know how to say *antihistamine* in Malay, and this was probably the last place you'd find it. I was losing it rapidly, and kept focusing on my breathing. At least I could breathe. I heard before that some bites or stings could cause the throat to swell and airways could be blocked. As far as I could feel, that wasn't happening to me. I could not move my leg though. Suddenly I felt my whole body being yanked up, several arms and hands all over me, my feet dragging across the ground. I tried to use my feet to get a grip on the floor, but could not. I could see I was being hoisted over the bridge and out of the village, by three people. I did my best to support my own weight now, as one leg came back to life. The other leg was still on fire. From the voices around me, all I could discern was *Pawai*. From that, I assumed they were taking me to the only person with a car around here, who would be able to drive to the hospital. As each moment passed, my head became clearer and I became more conscious of what was going on. I came around properly as I was sat in the back of Pawai's car, hurtling along the road. I dare not move my leg as the pain only increased each time. I started to wonder what on earth would have stung or bitten me to cause this.

After some time we arrived at Kudat hospital, and I was attended to. I am not sure what was said, but asked in English what had happened. There wasn't much to say. One minute I was fine, the next, not. I caught some of the conversation the Doctor had with Pawai and my fellow carriers from the village, and understood part of it to involve some flying insect which had entered the room, apparently. It was something known to cause a lot of pain, and I had had a particularly bad reaction to it. Here I was given some kind of antihistamine and simply sent back to the car. Although I still couldn't use one leg, it seemed that no one was alarmed that much anymore. I wasn't sure whether I should be reassured or not by that, but I had an engagement ceremony to attend tomorrow, so thought maybe it was best to hobble back to the village. And that is what I did.

By the next morning, the pain had subsided surprisingly, and I could actually feel my foot again. I was able to move around, albeit with a limp. Not the best timing but at least all the other symptoms had gone.

I could see that there were many people going in and out of Sabrinah's house during the day, preparing things for this evening's event. I had no idea what to expect, I hadn't even seen a wedding let alone an engagement ceremony. At least I would get to see Sabrinah's house this time.

Evening came around and I had dressed in the smartest clothes I had, which weren't much. Long slacks and a collared long sleeve shirt was all. I was taken over to Sabrinah's house where everyone was waiting. As I entered the living area of the house, I could see that it was a large sized room, with a small coffee table in the middle. No chairs or any other furniture to be seen. Lots of people, including Sabrinah and her father and brother, were sat around the periphery of the room. Pawai was also there, as the main witness and translator. I was not to sit next to Sabrinah at this point, but on the opposite side of the room. It was dark outside, and the room was lit by several candles. This gave the whole occasion a very ancient and traditional feel, which I felt was very fitting for some reason. There was again a lot of talk, which I did not understand, but the tone was gentle and included a lot of smiles and laughter. There would be no more rude interruptions here.

Finally came the agreed details which was relayed to me by Pawai. Before the actual wedding day, I was to pay a set amount of money, for the dowry, which would be used to pay for the wedding ceremony itself. On top of that, I needed to give one buffalo and two pigs to my new father-in-law, and make a promise to 'look after' him once I was married. This last part was important, since the only person to look after him since his wife, Sabrinah's mother, had passed away some years ago, Sabrinah was the only person to take care of him into his old age. This was straight forward and easy for me to agree to. There was no old age care system in this part of the world, it was completely upon the children to look after their parents right to the end. I was fine with that, and never like the western idea of care homes anyway. As for the buffalo and pigs, I knew that I would get help to find and get a good purchase for those. I learned that the pigs were for the wedding feast itself - as an extremely important sacrificial role, pigs were always used in Rungus culture. Other cultures across Borneo did the same, with chickens or goats, usually. The buffalo, however, would be used essentially as a tractor - to pull the plough in the paddy fields - and a very valued asset amongst Rungus people. Included in the agreement was the date of the wedding, set by Sabrinah herself. It was to be July in the following summer.

Once all the formalities were over, there were a couple of things that Pawai had up his sleeve. Firstly, he decided it was a fine opportunity for a photo. Knowing I was the only person to have a camera, and that I was so focused on the event itself, he guessed I would forget to take a picture of the momentous event. At this point Sabrinah and I both got up and stood together for a photo. Once that was taken, he suddenly declared to everyone that by western traditions, the fiancee should kiss the fiance. Regardless of that being true or not, it was his way of saying that things are done differently in the west. To my surprise, Sabrinah turned to me and quickly gave me a kiss on the cheek. And with that, we were engaged.

The Return

Sabah is known as the *Land Below the Wind*, so called because it lies south of the typhoon belt. It felt like all of the struggles that both Sabrinah and I had been through, finally seemed to be blown away. It felt like we reached an inevitable point in our two paths, that was always going to happen. Despite the attempts made by the Chief's family, and despite my own beliefs faltering, we had done it.

And just as it had all come together, my own time was running out. I had two days before my flight out of Sabah. I had been reassured that I need not worry anymore about interference or jealousy from other families. The entire village had come together to accept that Sabrinah and I had become engaged. Pawai reinforced this point to me as I said my last goodbye to him.

"Do not worry, Sam. Everything is fine now - your engagement with Sabrinah is a very serious matter and will not be challenged anymore. You've both done it! I will keep an eye on things for you here anyway. I wish you all the best."

He left to return to his house that night, after promising to keep in touch by letter, and be a go between when I needed to contact Sabrinah whilst I was in the UK. Of course, there were no phones out here to receive my call, and certainly no email.

Written letter was the only feasible way to communicate, and Pawai happened to have a more reliable address to send mail to. It highlighted the next challenge Sabrinah and I would face - to be apart on either side of the world, with the only hope of any communication being letters sent by airmail. Hopefully that would work. Coming back in July meant seven months. I knew we could do this.

The morning came when I had to leave. My backpack was packed the night before, and dutifully carried by Mosuta to where the truck would pick me up. Sabrinah walked with me across the bridge, as we slowly made our way to where Mosuta was waiting. She asked me about the life I was returning to, what I would do until returning here. I hadn't given it much thought. No-one back home knew what I had gone through. Bro and Seb were the only friends I had that knew I went back to the village , and that I had met someone. I'm sure they would be pretty surprised to hear what happened though. And of course my own family. How would they take the news? Putting that to one side, I told Sabrinah my intention was to return to my 'village', and find a job to save some money, before returning to Sabah. She planned to return to KK to do the same.

So here we were, having to say goodbye for seven months, after literally one day of being engaged. We stopped on the wooden walkway before it turned a corner. We held hands, and looked at each other. So much of what we both felt was communicated through looks and not words. Whilst this might be common for many people, in our case we had no choice. Neither of us had the vocabulary we needed. As I made a mental note to buy a Malay to English dictionary once in the UK, Sabrinah kissed me again on the cheek, said goodbye, and turned back toward the village. I watched her as she walked on, then turned myself, and continued on to meet Mosuta at the bus stop. The truck was waiting for me, to take me on the first part of my long trip back to the UK.

Later that day, in KK airport for one more time, I felt the wheels of the plane leave the tarmac. I had a similar but different feeling to the last time this happened. A promise to Sabrinah that I would return, as I did before. But this time, we were engaged. How different that felt! I thought about the months to come. What I would do? And what would I do when I return to Sabah and finally get married? So typical of me, I literally had no plan. But whatever it was, I knew it would turn out OK. If I had to clean toilets for a living in the Centre Point mall in KK, I would.

I went through in my mind all the possessions I had in the UK, what I could sell to raise money to pay for the wedding. I had to buy a buffalo and two pigs after all. Would selling my old VW van raise enough for that? It would be an interesting challenge. It didn't take long for me to sleep, and on this rare occasion, I didn't wake up until the plane was only a few miles out from a much colder London.

Mum and Dad had come down to Heathrow to meet me. It was great to see my parents again. Both were happy to see me again too - Mum was her usual emotional self, and Dad just grinning as he always did. I had been away for less than a year, but because of the remote location I was in, and such a contrasting environment, it made the time seem much longer. I was hearing English everywhere. People were walking at a much faster speed. I had read about reverse culture shock, now

I was feeling it. On top of that, I was tired. I decided not to break the big news until we got home.

Home. A nice fitting, solid front door, carpeted hallways and living room. Books on shelves. Funny, the things I started to notice. My mind still clearly not caught up with my physical presence in the UK. I think it was still swimming around in the warm sea, next to that deserted beach.

Mum did her usual, and got the kettle on. We sat around the kitchen table with our cups of English tea - something I hadn't had for seemingly ages. I took out some photos I had already developed. Naturally, Mum and Dad wanted to know all about the expedition, and my travels afterwards. Pictures help the stories. We went through many photos, I did my best to fit in the stories associated with each one. Many of course were of the village itself, and I could not imagine how those pictures would come across. I had lived there, and no photo could do any justice to the uniqueness of the place that was so special to me now.

"You must have really liked this village if you went back to visit after the expedition," my mum commented, looking at the bridge, the jungle, and the photos of many of the Rungus people. I could tell she was suspecting something. Mums can be so intuitive, and this one was no exception.

"Yes, absolutely. But I need to go back again," I declared. Mum and dad looked up from the photos in their hands, now looking at me.

"There's a young couple getting married in the village, and they invited me to their wedding," I continued, "I have to go, I promised. It will be a big traditional wedding, quite amazing to witness I should think. I have a photo of the couple here."

I passed them a photo I had been holding back. It was one of Sabrinah and I, standing in front of a tree in the village. Mum looked at the photo and covered her mouth, eyes watering.

"I knew it!" she said, trying to hold back the tears. She passed the photo to dad, who looked at it and just grinned.

Epilogue

My story began standing on the bridge, across the water, below the wind, wearing my beaded straps and that green polyester suit. And here it will end.

But just to give a *little* bit more: this moment on the bridge, in my ill-fitting suit, was on our wedding day itself. I'd sold my van, earned a bit of money, and said farewell to all my family in the UK. Not knowing what would happen, I had no idea at the time when I might return.

I crossed the bridge, escorted by Pawai and his family, to enter the village and meet Sabrinah, waiting for me in the village church. People from many other villages in the district had also come to see the wedding take place. News had spread that a foreigner and a local girl were to marry. Half of them needed to see it to believe it. They had plenty of time - the wedding lasted three days.

I was now to refer to Kikiek, my father-in-law, as *Ivan (pronounced "Eee Van"* - I was not allowed to use his actual name, since I was now a member of the family). He was very happy with the buffalo. And I learned that Sabrinah actually had six brothers, not one. The other five had not been in the village for a few years. I had just never met them before. I asked her why she never told me that she had more than one brother. She just shrugged and said, "well, you never asked!"

Pawai told me that day, on the bridge, to write this book. I did. Actually, many people back home told me to do the same, once they heard about one or two anecdotes of my travels. I'm glad they all told me. It motivated me. I guess some parts of it seemed interesting to some- even the UK media somehow picked up on our wedding. The *Yorkshire Post* did a full page article on Sabrinah and I, telling the tale of an engineering graduate who built a bridge in the jungle, and bought a pig and a buffalo as part of his wedding. I guess it *is* an unusual story.

That story was then picked up by *The Sun* newspaper, which was then discussed briefly on *BBC Radio 1*. I know this, because Seb, who was working as an interior decorator at the time, nearly dropped his brush in surprise as my name was mentioned on his work radio. He called me to tell me this. When I received the call, I was sitting in our new home in Kota Kinabalu. A place that my new employer had provided for us, the first home Sabrinah and I had.

In Beverly Hills Apartments, Sabah. The Land Below the Wind.

Printed in Great Britain
by Amazon

48797631R00111